Sex, Love and Who Puts the Rubbish Out?

How the Philosophy of 9-Energy Natural Expression Helps You
Understand Your Relationships and Brings Happiness to Your Life

RICK NUNN

Copyright © 2016 Rick Nunn.

All rights reserved. No part of this book may be reproduced, stored, or transmitted by any means—whether auditory, graphic, mechanical, or electronic—without written permission of both publisher and author, except in the case of brief excerpts used in critical articles and reviews. Unauthorized reproduction of any part of this work is illegal and is punishable by law.

ISBN: 978-1-4834-5432-0 (sc)
ISBN: 978-1-4834-5433-7 (e)

Library of Congress Control Number: 2016946091

Because of the dynamic nature of the Internet, any web addresses or links contained in this book may have changed since publication and may no longer be valid. The views expressed in this work are solely those of the author and do not necessarily reflect the views of the publisher, and the publisher hereby disclaims any responsibility for them.

Any people depicted in stock imagery provided by Thinkstock are models, and such images are being used for illustrative purposes only. Certain stock imagery © Thinkstock.

Rev. date: 8/8/2016

To the people I love, especially Charlie my daughter.

CONTENTS

Introduction ix
How on earth did I get here?

Part 1: Living through Nature

1   Ignore Gurus, Best Friends and Self-Help Books. 1
Everything you're told is a lie... until you prove it correct for yourself.

2   So Who Does Put the Rubbish Out? 3
Yang is from Mars, Yin is from Venus

3   Behind every Successful Yang, there's a Successful Yin 7
Relationships that are at One with each other

4   Why Peeling Onions Makes you Cry. 9
Your 9-Energy Natural Expression is who you really are

5   There really is a Third Person in your Relationship! 13
Looking after No 3

6   And so they lived Happily Ever After - Apart 15
Why Learned Convention is bunk

7   Out of 8.7 million breeds of animals, only 11 mate for Life:
Humans aren't included. 19
Better to break the rules, than be broken by them

8	Resistance is Futile 21
	So give up, let go and be happy

9	The Only Way Not to get Hurt in Love 23
	Letting go of attachments

10	You want Unconditional Love?. 27
	Just make sure you read the small print

Part 2: The world of 9-Energy Natural Expression

1	Before we get started. 31

2	What actually is 9-Energy Natural Expression?. 33

3	How Yin and Yang, 5 phases, 5 elements, 4 seasons and the 9 family members all fit in. 37

4	Working out your 9-Energy Natural Expression. 47

5	Revealing your 9-Energy Natural Expression 53

6	Relationships 127

And finally.... 223
References 225
Bibliography 227
What next? 229

INTRODUCTION

How on earth did I get here?

It all started one Saturday morning. My then partner and I were having, how I can say it, 'difficulties' and we were on the way to attend our first counselling session. I loved her very much, and I believed she loved me too, and we wanted this relationship to work. To be honest, there was quite a back story between us with two goes at this relationship spanning 20 years or so and worthy of any corny Hollywood rom-com. I was sad that our relationship had come to this again, but optimistic too that this time we could work our way through it.

We were driving to a town called Stony Stratford, an hour or so out of London, and the journey was in stony silence which seemed sort of apt. I knew virtually nothing about the person we were going to see. What I did know was that he was 'alternative'. She didn't want us to see anyone from Relate[1] or a western qualified counsellor, and that was fine because the truth was that I was happy to follow her lead, especially if that meant a better chance of this working.

On the journey up, and with clearly nothing to talk about, I couldn't help but think of previous counselling sessions I'd had in a past relationship. The vast majority of which were fraught to say the least. But you see we were angry with each other, suspicious and weary. It had got to the stage where we really just wanted to let off steam to a third party with the sole motive of getting them to see just how difficult and unreasonable the other one was and just how patient, kind and understanding we were. Or at least that's how it was for me. But this time it was different, I wanted this to work, and we were going to be open and responsive to whatever insights were going to be offered. Or at least that's how it was for me...

---

[1] The UK's largest provider of relationship support

His house was tucked away at the end of a modern estate and a tall, middle aged man opened the door, smiled and shook our hands. No obvious tattoos, piercings or pony tails and he was casually dressed in the sort of clothes I'd wear if I didn't really care what I was wearing. No waft of incense greeted us and the hallway looked boringly normal, the rooms I could see from the hallway looked normal, the pictures were normal, the knick-knacks were normal, he looked normal. OK, there was nothing 'alternative' going on here. It was all, how can I put it, normal.

We followed him up the stairs and turned left into a little room with what looked like two glorified deckchairs, a treatment couch and a small stool. We looked around, not quite sure where to go. Was this a test? He waved us towards the chairs and he perched himself, quite literally, on the stool. This is more like it I thought, a little less normal and a bit more alternative, although not that much alternative to be honest.

In my experience of the more 'traditional' counselling I had in that previous relationship, I've realised that getting your retaliation in first is crucial. You need to get your side of the story out there as soon as possible and paint a picture of injustice, hurt and bewilderment. You need to sound reasonable and calm, whilst at the same time making it quite obvious to even the most myopic of counsellors whose side they should be on i.e. yours. When it's your turn to do the listening, or the pretence of listening, a slight but fixed furrow of the eyebrows, micro shakings of the head and low sighs are all acceptable means to rubbish the other side's view of events.

Yes, I can see now that perhaps I didn't really go into those particular counselling sessions with the right frame of mind. Sorry to the person concerned but you see one of the problems of counselling is that by the time you get there, your relationship is usually not just on the rocks, but already bits of driftwood dispersed widely along the seashore. Sadly, it's often all too late and the love you once had for your partner is now something that you just remember, like an idyllic childhood holiday you once had, but perhaps on reflection you never did. Also the counsellor rarely says what they are really thinking and won't give an opinion. "So how does that make you feel?", "What do you think?" "What are you hearing here?" can only go so far before frustration and exhaustion make you want to scream. But the real problem of 'traditional' counselling is that it can take an age to really get to know the people involved and what's actually going on and then how something positive can be done about it. And many never get there, despite all the time and the money – and the tears.

I was brought out of my reverie when the counsellor turned to me first:
"So, Rick, why don't you tell me what's going on?"

Ah, so I was going to be allowed to fire the first shots: funny, because now I really didn't want to go first. I loved this woman way too much to want to hurt her intentionally or otherwise, but I gave my 10 minutes' worth, taking the blame for most of the contentious issues and then it was her turn. I don't recall her having quite the same self-blame quotient as me, but her take on it all didn't sound that unreasonable. Not many notes were taken; in fact I'm not sure if any were. She didn't hog her time in the spotlight and soon it was silent. And then we waited.

I suppose in the scheme of things, most of us don't have that many life-changing moments. But this was certainly going to be one of mine. The counsellor then spent the next half hour or so, maybe less, describing *exactly* what was going on for me, going on for her, and going on for us in the relationship. When he finished, I was wondering if this was actually a Derren Brown[2] trick and that we were being secretly filmed. We just gave him the headlines, but he gave us the in-depth expose.

As we drove away I was asked what I made of all that. "It was amazing" I said. "It was like a Derren Brown trick. Do you think we were being secretly filmed?"

"Yes" she said, "he really did talk my language. But there was one thing he did want to know before we came today, and I didn't want to tell you what it was."

"Uh..huh, what was that then?", I asked suspiciously.

"He wanted to know our birthdates".

There was a long pause.

"Yes, I'm glad you didn't tell me that", and before I could say any more, she finished my sentence: "because you wouldn't have come if you had known that, would you?"

She was right; someone telling me such personal things based on the day I was born? Not a cat's chance in hell.

But it was the start of a journey I'm still on today and likely to be on for the rest of my life. Sadly, I didn't start the journey early enough to save our relationship for I soon came to realise that I had been 'playing a part' not just in this relationship, but generally in my life. And for the most part, it simply wasn't me. We went together a few more times even after we split,

---

[2] Derren Brown is an English mentalist and illusionist.

but soon I started to go on my own. I needed to; the break-up left me in a dreadful state and at times in a very dark and dangerous one. Up to this point, it seemed that I had lost everything. Redundancies from two high paying jobs in the advertising industry less than 18 months apart and as a consequence of the failed 'traditional' counselling sessions I described earlier, an on-going divorce from hell that had left me both mentally broken and financially ruined.

As for the love of my life? How can the same person completely shatter your heart twice in a lifetime? Everyone has their own sob story, but it seemed to me that my place on this earth really wasn't worth very much.

At first, my visits to Stony Stratford were simply counselling: it made me feel better and at times his help and words almost seemed to save my life. He introduced me to a whole new and different world which I just lapped up. It was full of captivating characters such as UG Krishnamurti, Douglas Harding, Masanobu Fukuoka and Tony Parsons (no, not the Man and Boy author); the wonders of natural farming in Japan; and living life 'as it is' or as if you had 'no head'. But underlining all this were the benefits of Traditional Chinese Medicine and specifically the mysterious world of 9-Energy Natural Expression. After a while, the sessions became less counselling and more learning and slowly, with his encouragement, it dawned on me that 9-Energy Natural Expression was something I naturally connected to and could offer its insight and benefits to others. It certainly seemed to work, and the friends I counselled to begin with seemed as amazed as I was by the staggering and often spookily accurate revelations it uncovered. It still amazes me today.

But as you explore this book, please bear in mind this: "Everything I tell you is a lie, until you prove it correct for yourself". I've no idea who said it first, and I'm not taking the credit, but it's true. It is of course a make-over of the Buddhist saying "Believe nothing, unless it agrees with your own reason". This sentiment is explored further in chapter one.

In one of the most brutal books I've ever read about the human condition 'Mind Is A Myth' by the previously mentioned U G Krishnamurti (with the wry subheading "Disquieting conversations with a man called UG", and you'd better believe they're disquieting!), he states that he's not trying to preach to anyone, but rather he's singing his song and if you want to listen to it, then do. If you don't, then don't. The principle here is the same. If this whole 9-Energy Natural Expression philosophy, concept, system - call it what you will - strikes a chord, then explore it further if you wish, but if it doesn't, then don't. Maybe one day it will, but it doesn't matter to me one way or the other, and I will never try to convince anyone or argue its case. It's either real for you or it's not: and both those options - and anything in between - are all absolutely fine.

So yes, you will need to make your own mind up if what is written holds true for you. This is my take on something that has been around for 5000 years or so, but 'updated' if you will, for the 21st century and made accessible and as relevant as possible to the way we live our lives today.

I've written this book in two parts.

The first part is how I see sex, love and relationships lived out through nature with 9-Energy Natural Expression as our guide and mentor. It would seem to me that for the vast majority of us that is not how we are living our lives. I think it is important to lay the foundations and these chapters provide background and texture to this whole philosophy.

Of course, if you want to skip to the second part then do so and it will be here that you'll find the nuts and bolts of working out your 9-Energy Natural Expression and how that manifests in you, the people in your life and the relationships you have with them. It will show you what will be natural, instinctive and intuitive in your love life, in the bedroom and yes who puts the rubbish out. That's a metaphor of course, but it's a neat way of setting out the dynamics of a relationship and determining who should be taking the lead and setting the boundaries. Knowing your 9-Energy Natural Expression is the key to unlocking the door into who you really are and where answers and meaning can be found. But it is just a key, and once used it has done its job, and can be thrown away. For some the key will not open the door and that will be where this particular story ends - at least for now. For others it will be the start of something that could be challenging for sure and definitely revealing, but ultimately enlightening and probably rather wonderful! I hope you enjoy the journey.

PART 1
Living through Nature

CHAPTER 1

Ignore Gurus, Best Friends and Self-Help Books

Everything you're told is a lie...
until you prove it correct for yourself.

I had lunch with a friend the other day who had just returned from a month long 'spiritual' trip to India. She was full of new ideas and seemed convinced that she had 'turned a corner', or rather turned yet another corner as I had heard similar tales of epiphany before. Despite being happy for her, I couldn't help wishing she would find her own way rather than following the latest whim of yet another guru, especially as this one claimed to be God. Interestingly the very attractive woman he married had a vision at an early age that one day she would marry God. It was lucky then that during their courtship he let slip that he was in fact God.

My friend had to find her own way to God's temple and whilst she admitted the accommodation and food were rather basic for $100 a night, the temple was impressive and God preached a good sermon or two. Well, quite a few actually, as the minimum stay was thirty nights. "And out of interest, how many people were there?" I asked.

"About 400," she said. Hmmm, not bad; God's raking in $1.2million a month plus all those little point-of-sale extras like books and trinkets that were surely close at hand. I can't imagine he paid his devoted helpers very much either, if at all. But in some ways, you can't blame these 'gurus' who claim this that and the other and charge you a pretty penny for the privilege. I mean they're not forcing you to part with your hard earned cash are they? Or maybe in some ways, they are. If you're dying from thirst, you'll drink water from anywhere. On balance though, all-knowing gurus are probably more concerned with their own well-being than yours.

But what about friends or family members to whom you might turn to for help or advice? You'd think it'd be an advantage that they know you and are likely to have a good idea of the situation you are facing be it with work, relationships, money or whatever. They certainly should be on your side. I have found that there are usually two things going on. First, because they are on your side, their help is inevitably going to be skewed. How can it not be? The two extremes are that they will agree with whatever your take is on the situation or they will play the classic 'cruel to be kind' or 'devil's advocate' cards. Second (and much harder to spot) is that their advice is so often really them advising themselves. When they say you should do this or that in a particular situation, what they are really saying is this is what they should have done or should do. You are just their mirror.

And self-help books? We can also add counsellors and therapists in this group. Again, like gurus and best friends, you're sure to find one to suit your particular needs at the time, and if you don't like what you are hearing or reading, well, just find another one until you do!

Now make no mistake, not for one moment am I saying that any of these sources of guidance and help are not to be taken notice of and despite the God guru described earlier, I really don't want to make any judgement on their motives or credibility. But what I am saying is that who or what we are drawn to depends so much on our state of mind at the time. What feels right today might not feel quite so right tomorrow. At the end of the day, all we are listening to or reading is the ego of the person delivering it: that is the key. It is all mind related, your state of mind engaging (and following) their state of mind.

It seems to me whatever 'journey' you are on, it shouldn't require that much mental effort or analysis - indeed no thought process at all really. You actually just need to let go and trust what your body is telling you, not your ego. If it feels naturally and instinctively right in your bones, it is right.

So yes, ignore gurus, best friends and self-help books – and experts, religious leaders and politicians, anyone really who purports to tell you what's best for you. It's all lies. And it only ever stops being a lie when you and your bones can prove it otherwise for yourself.

Let's finish with this wonderful quote from Nisargdatta Maharaj, who Wikipedia describes as an Indian guru! Oh well!

"When you deceive yourself that you work for the good of all,
it makes matters worse,
for you should not be guided by your own ideas of what is good for others.
A man who claims to know what is good for others,
is dangerous."

CHAPTER 2

So Who Does Put the Rubbish Out?

Yang is from Mars, Yin is from Venus

In my early 40's, I remember my partner at the time solemnly handing me the book 'Men are from Mars, Women are from Venus'. "Read this", she growled, "and then you'll understand." I did as I was told and John Gray's self-help book remains one of the few of its kind that I actually read from cover to cover. Amongst the many observations and advice two things stuck: men like to retreat into their caves when the going gets tough and women actually just want to talk about their problems and not have unsolicited attempts by men trying to solve them.

They stuck, like most things that do, because they had resonance with me. They still do, but the problem I had then, and only resolved recently, was that I knew plenty of women who withdrew to an unapproachable place at the first sniff of trouble and many men who just wanted to talk about their problems without interruption or unwanted advice. It seemed I knew plenty of 'types' who retreated into caves and plenty of other 'types' who preferred to talk rather than do. So clearly this wasn't a gender thing, but I could see that there were definitely common patterns of behaviour. So what was going on?

I found the answer in a book called the *I Ching* or *Book of Changes* written in ancient China many thousands of years ago. I will go into this in more detail later, but all you need to know for now is that back then the sages were also observing that certain groups of people shared similar behaviours and characteristics and found that whilst there were indeed two equal but opposite forces governing humanity it wasn't a male and female thing, but what they called a Yin and Yang thing.

Now this seemed to make sense because the more I observed people the more I found that the primary difference was not being male or female but being Yin or Yang. Of course there are the physical aspects between the sexes that manifest in certain behaviours, but this is not at a person's core. Instead that is sourced from the predominance of Yin or Yang within them and that has little to do with gender.

I will go into a lot more detail about Yin and Yang during the course of the book, but here is a flavour of what Yin and Yang is all about:

1. All phenomena contain two innate but opposing forces
2. Yin and Yang are co-dependent
3. Yin and Yang nurture each other
4. Yin and Yang creates Oneness

Generally, you could say that in humans, Yang is loud and hard, has lots to say, is pushy, insensitive and wants to lead and have things their own way. Yin is quiet and soft, has less to say, is sensitive and will tend to follow and compromise. Now it's really important to understand that no one is 100% Yang or 100% Yin, but we are made up of different proportions.

This is represented brilliantly in the YinYang symbol that will be familiar to many.

You will see the different thickness or quantities of the black (Yin) and the white (Yang) as you move around the circle and within each half there is a spot of the opposite colour or force.

This phenomenon of Yin and Yang applies to all of nature, not just humanity, and this is what can be called the Natural World. Its opposite is the Un-Natural world or what I describe as 'Learned Convention'. It is similar to the on-going debate about personalities and behaviours being conditioned by either nature or nurture.

It is Learned Convention that 'tells' us that men should behave one way and women the other and we've unwittingly allowed ourselves to be ruled and judged by this convention. It starts early, typically parents will clothe their baby boys in blue and give them toy cars to play with and dress their girls in pink and encourage them to play with dolls. As the children get older, they will observe how their parents behave towards each other and the gender specific roles they tend to take (who does the ironing or the DIY, who prepares the BBQ and who cooks it, who practices yoga or who pumps iron – the examples are endless). When they start schooling and mature into adults, these sexual stereotypes are often reinforced by teachers, peer groups and the media.

So Learned Convention will tell us that it's the man's job to put the rubbish out. Now of course, I'm using this to make a point and it's not necessary to take this seriously or literally, but it does neatly define a typical masculine role. In our world and the relationships we have, we tend to comply and reinforce these masculine and feminine roles and traits, hence the fertile ground of 'Men are from Mars and Women are from Venus.' In actual fact, and still using the same metaphors, it's not men who are from Mars and put the rubbish out - but Yang!

You'll be able to find out in Part 2 of the book if you're Yin or Yang, but before then, let's explore how this phenomenon manifests itself in our relationships.

CHAPTER 3

Behind every Successful Yang, there's a Successful Yin

Relationships that are at One with each other

OK, before we go any further, let me nail down what I mean by 'success'. It is not the high fives, fist pumping, whooping type of success. It's not a competitive 'winning' kind of success at the expense of someone else. Nor is it a success involving overcoming great odds or difficulties. No, it's the success of just being who you really are, requiring no effort or grand strategy. You'd think that would be pretty easy, and it is, if only we can switch off our minds and forget all about Learned Convention!

In the previous chapter, I gave an overview on the traits of Yin and Yang (and in Part 2, I go into more detail), but it's important to stress that in the world of 9-Energy Natural Expression, there is no such thing as a good or bad relationship: if a relationship works, it works and that's the end of it! Nevertheless, Yin and Yang is all about balance and if your relationship has a YinYang fit, it will be a smoother combination than if it hasn't, but that doesn't necessarily make it a better relationship. In this chapter I am going to explore further the importance of this YinYang fit, why it works and what happens when it doesn't.

Now, in essence, it is natural for Yang to want to be seen and to lead. Being 'seen' for who they are is a big part of their being and in the YinYang world they are the stars (both of the celestial kind and the metaphoric kind). But stars can only be seen if there is a dark night behind them. And that dark night is Yin. In a rock band, Yang is the lead guitar and the singer, Yin is the rhythm section - the bass and drums. In the world of James Bond, Yang is the martini, Yin is the ice. So whilst you can obviously have one without the other, it doesn't really work. I mean a warm martini? And in terms of gender, Yang is male and Yin is female.

Now here's the rub and it is counter-intuitive in the modern world where the power and dominance of Yang is seen to be more relevant: Yang actually needs Yin more than Yin needs Yang. Ironically Yang doesn't believe that and neither does Yin! But for YinYang to be of nature and for the wellbeing of us all, this basic premise has to be observed. Not in a competitive way of one being more important or better than the other (they are not) but just in the natural way of things.

So, the actual starting point is Yin. If Yin people are not living as Yin this is what happens. They feel like victims, insignificant, unimportant, not worth being listened to or they believe they should behave in a Yang way and try to become dominant and loud and to win at all costs. Both states are catastrophic for Yin. In those circumstances and without the stability of Yin, Yang goes off the rails. They become even more Yang: more competitive, aggressive and unyielding in their beliefs and views. They will abuse the Yin, which they perceive to be weak, but it's not Yin being weak, it's just Yin not being Yin.

When Yin starts to live their Natural Expression and just be, without seeking or needing the approval of others (especially Yang) and feels comfortable and at ease in themselves and their place in the world, then Yang can relax and become less of the ego-mind and lead naturally as it is supposed to do. Yin doesn't have to do anything and should avoid going towards the Yang, but simply be there to guide and advise when asked. And Yang will ask, and Yang must listen. It might not take the course of action Yin has suggested, at least not straight away, but it needs Yin, and probably more than the Yin will ever know.

In relationships, it can be very hard for Yang to understand Yin and vice versa. But really understanding isn't as important as just knowing when it feels right, as too much analysis is often a bad thing. When Yin struggles, it tends to go either further inwards or towards the Yang to seek direction and inspiration. Unless asked, Yang should avoid trying to solve Yin's problems, but instead just listen. It will try to come up with solutions because that's what Yang does, but it mustn't try to impose anything because that will usually make things worse for Yin, and when it gets bad for Yin, it's going to get bad for Yang.

So the expression we use of course is that behind every successful man, there stands a woman. But this is not so much a man and woman thing, but a Yin and Yang thing. When Yin and Yang connect, as they are meant to do and must, it creates a relationship that is at 'One'.

CHAPTER 4

Why Peeling Onions Makes you Cry

Your 9-Energy Natural Expression is who you really are

The same partner who introduced me to 'Men are from Mars, Women are from Venus' soon became my wife and one of the delightful 'extras' she brought to our relationship were her two wonderful sons aged 4 and 6. They were bright, well-mannered and great fun to be with and it was a privilege to play a part in their upbringing. Their getting-ready-to-go-to-school routine was always pretty hectic and often chaotic and I remember one such morning when I was on the school-run and trying to hurry up the younger one to get ready.

"OK, so we need to get going in about 10 minutes, so finish off that game and start to get your stuff". He continues to play his game. A few minutes pass. "I told you to stop playing and get ready for school. Now where did you leave your shoes and have you got your bag?" He runs to the front door to where he thinks he left his shoes, but they're not there; unconcerned he goes back to his game. As for his bag, he's pretty sure he's given it to Alex because Alex wanted it and he likes Alex. More minutes pass. "Right we really are going to be late now! Where are your shoes? Aren't they by the door? Oh no wait, I cleaned them last night, they'll be in the kitchen, but where's your bag? What do you mean you gave it to Alex?! He can't be your best friend; I thought you hated him because he took your book and made you cry. Don't you remember? And please hurry up!"

He doesn't remember, and if he did he wouldn't care; all he knows is that Alex is his new best friend. And there may have been a timetable ticking for me but there wasn't for him.

Parents often find it hard to understand why their 4 year old won't hurry up when asked and appears to have no concept of time. Or how someone who was a sworn enemy the day before is now their best chum. They in turn would struggle to understand why their parents always seem to be in a rush and if he likes Alex today, what's the big deal if he didn't like him yesterday? In the world of 9-Energy Natural Expression, it's the child who's got it right, not that he either knows or cares – and that's how it should be.

Your 9-Energy Natural Expression and how that manifests in the real world is explored in detail in Part 2, but all you need to know for now is that your 9-Energy Natural Expression is who you were as a child aged around 3 to 5, unencumbered by the Learned Convention I spoke about in Chapter 2 or with fears about the future or angst about the past.

Of course it's hard, probably impossible to remember how we were as a 4 year old, but back then we really did live in the moment and took life just as we found it. Our judgements on people and events were based upon the here and now and we asked questions because we wanted to know the answer with no concept of being tactful so as not to upset anyone. If we are having fun and liking someone, why on earth should we care if we didn't like them yesterday or spend one second thinking if we were going to like them tomorrow?

We might then say that our 4 year old's Natural Expression is like the core of an onion. But as we get older what happens to our little onion? Learned Convention and 'lessons in life', that's what happens, and each one of these experiences either adds a layer to the onion or thickens the ones that are already there. This all comes from the mind or ego, and so before long many of us have grown into a huge, tough, impressive looking onion or Ego-Onion and that soft core is buried under layers and layers of life's experiences. We end up living our lives from the surface, maybe shedding and revealing a layer or two to our loved ones, but we stop living our lives as our Natural Expression and who we really are and that naïve, innocent, curious little 4 year old is lost.

It's time then to start peeling the Ego-Onion.

Obviously, the bigger your Ego-Onion the more layers that need to be peeled away before your core 9-Energy Natural Expression can be revealed. Of course for many, the last thing they want is to reveal their true selves, for who knows what they might find? We may feel ill at ease and not particularly happy with our lot, but we reason it's our lot, and it's familiar and we can draw some comfort from that. It's often much easier for instance to stay put in an unfulfilling job or an unhappy relationship than to change.

The whole point about 9-Energy Natural Expression is that it reveals who you actually are and not who you think you are; neither does it have anything to do with the events in your life that you may believe define you for good or ill. These are the layers of your Ego-Onion that need to be removed and that will probably be painful and make you cry.

The tears that are shed come from so many different places: mainly of regret and frustration of leading a life that just wasn't you and the sadness and futility of judging people and events selfishly and without consideration and being judged similarly in return for being someone you're not. The bottom line is simply a misunderstanding and an unwitting ignorance of what your Natural Expression actually means. Once that is understood, accepted and acted upon, the tears of suffering will turn to tears of relief and joy.

CHAPTER 5

There really is a Third Person in your Relationship!
Looking after No 3

When two people fall in love and connect with each other, they often say it feels like they've created 'something special'. Not all couples feel that of course, but either way it is true that when two people get together something new is created, and this is the Third Person or Energy in your relationship.

In the world of 9-Energy Natural Expression you can be in one of 3 kinds of relationships: Opposites, Parent & Child or Friends and you'll need to refer to the Relationships chapter in Part 2 to find out more about this and what kind of relationship you're in. Don't get hung up on the terminology or take anything too literally or think that one relationship type is better than the other – they are not. The key thing here is that each type creates a new and different relationship - the No 3. In some cases this No 3 relationship is greater than the sum of your individual parts; sometimes less, sometimes the same but all three of you in the relationship is no more or less important than any of the others – all are equal. It is worth noting at this point that whilst this chapter is focussing on 'romantic' one-to-one relationships this refers to *all* types of relationships, so it's equally relevant for personal and professional relationships as well.

It is often said that for a healthy relationship, each individual should have their own friends and interests separate from their partners and then, as a couple, you should have shared friends and interests. If the relationship is in difficulties then this is something you should definitely look at because it's likely that the dynamics between the 3 forces in your relationship are out of balance. This is not prescriptive to a successful relationship; I have seen many happy couples who appear to have no shared interests whatsoever whilst others seem to do everything together. The main thing though is to recognise the presence of the No 3 in your relationship.

So just as you would love, honour and respect your partner, so the same criteria should be directed towards the Relationship. This has nothing to do with the amount of time or effort you put into it, indeed, if more effort simply results in more difficulties or resistance then there is clearly something wrong. People will often tell you that you must work at a relationship and constantly find compromise. If that approach is natural for you both, and creates happiness and harmony then that's the right approach. If, on the other hand, it makes one or both of you resentful and unhappy then obviously it isn't.

The analogy I like to use is a three legged table with each leg representing you, your partner and the Relationship. It only takes one leg to be of a different length relative to the others for it to be unstable. So if you think you are more important than your partner (or vice versa) then that table is unlikely to stay up for long and if you think the Relationship doesn't require as much nurturing and consideration as the two of you, again it's going to wobble. Sometimes it helps to actually imagine the Relationship as an energy or force in the same room with you sitting there not doing or saying anything but at the same time knowing everything!

Peace, harmony and happiness will be found if you live your life as your 9-Energy Natural Expression, 'allow' your partner to do the same, and embrace whatever type of relationship you are in. You can't change this, it is what it is. If you are having difficulties, you may think with more effort and/or luck things can be turned around and your mind may create the illusion that for a while it is, but it is unsustainable and in the long term it will cause suffering and may even make you ill. No, the answer is to let go and love the fact that having relationships that truly connect is a privilege and a genuine force of nature.

CHAPTER 6

And so they lived Happily Ever After - Apart

Why Learned Convention is bunk

Learned Convention is a continuing theme of this book and one of the biggest, as far as couples' relationships are concerned, is the concept that we should live together under the same roof and when we do to share the same bedroom. Now of course there are plenty of couples who do neither and have a perfectly happy and harmonious relationship, but that's the blueprint and for many it can actually be a cause of much stress and even suffering in a relationship. The other big one is being monogamous and I consider that in more detail in the next chapter.

We form this sense of conformity to the norm early in our lives, and as I described previously, it soon becomes our Learned Convention. My daughter for instance, when aged 14, told me she would *never* ask a boy out and I asked her why. "Oh Daddy, you just don't understand, girls don't do that sort of thing". As my daughter is Yang that's exactly what she should be doing and when she's older she should be putting the rubbish out! To be fair my daughter likes convention or tradition as she would call it and there is absolutely nothing wrong with that. However waiting to be asked is more Yin behaviour and as that is not her Natural Expression it will just be adding more layers on her Ego-Onion. Whilst again there is nothing wrong with this, if she suppresses her natural Yang characteristics for any length of time, it could start to cause her suffering and unhappiness.

The same thing is likely to happen if you try to ignore or suppress the type of relationship you are in. One such case was a couple who were in what's known as a 'Conflict Opposites' relationship. (See Part 2, Chapter 6). Now remember, as far as 9-Energy Natural Expression is concerned, there is no such thing as a good or bad relationship despite this rather ominous sounding description! But this is what was happening to them and how it was that Learned Convention was at the root of their suffering.

This couple were in a tempestuous relationship. They were both in their early 30's, held down high powered jobs and worked long hours. They had one child, a boy aged 5. It was a very physical relationship in more ways than one. Their lovemaking was passionate and frequent but post-coitally they soon started to bicker which more often than not would lead to furious arguments, every bit as passionate as the sex they had just enjoyed. Usually they would make up with more sex, but equally as often either one or the other would leave the family home to spend a few days with friends and family until things cooled down. They would then get back together, declare undying love, have sex, fight, leave, get back together and so it went on. They knew damage was being done, especially to their son, and wanted to find a way to have a 'normal' relationship, but ultimately they felt the only solution was to split up.

They were right.

What they didn't know was that this pattern of behaviour was them simply playing out an aspect of their 9-Energy Natural Expression. Both were powerful Yang Expressions and with their relationship being a Conflict Opposites one, they needed space, and lots of it! But the problem was that they were creating this space by having these huge arguments and splitting up. They were doing it un-Naturally.

"So why don't you stay together but live apart and have separate homes?" I suggested. "I mean you can both afford it. Clearly you do love each other, but you have to realise and acknowledge that you need space from one another. And that's OK, there is nothing wrong with that; it's actually exactly what your 9-Energy Natural Expression is saying you both need. So enjoy your time together, but rather than wait for the inevitable explosion, create the space you both need naturally. And you do that by one of you going back to your own home."

"But we're married", they protested "and married couples are supposed to live together!"

Who says?

Learned Convention that's who; and it's a nonsense. Why does being married have to mean living under the same roof? It doesn't, and in this case it was causing them huge amounts of unhappiness and suffering and if left to continue would inevitably have led to the break-up of their family.

For many of us having two homes is a luxury we think we can't afford, although in reality that would be the inevitable consequence.

The point I'm trying to make is that we often do what we think looks right not only for ourselves, but for an external audience such as friends and family who can be swift to pass judgement. We end up getting so entrenched in a particular pattern of behaviour that we lose sight of what is actually Natural for us as individuals and as a couple. These Ego-Onions I speak about become so huge and unwieldy that they take on a life of their own. Often it takes a disaster, a break-down or some other type of calamity for the layers to be stripped away, but it doesn't have to be like that. Returning to your core Natural Expression means releasing the ego and rejecting Learned Convention - and the only thing that will try to resist that is your mind.

CHAPTER 7

Out of 8.7 million breeds of animals, only 11 mate for Life[3]: Humans aren't included

Better to break the rules, than be broken by them

I remember being in the depth of a relationship crisis some years back, and wailing to my counsellor that this latest break-up was an absolute tragedy because we were 'meant to be together'. I recalled saying that if swans can mate for life, why couldn't we? "Because we're not swans", he rather brutally replied. He then went on to tell me about a couple he had been counselling and the reaction of their little boy to one of his father's 'indiscretions'. It turned out that the 4 year old had secretly witnessed his Dad kissing another woman and rather than saying anything at the time, brought it up at breakfast the next day.

"Daddy, why were you kissing that woman last night?"

His father denied it, but the boy's mother had long suspected that something was going on and all hell broke loose. As the argument and shouting intensified, he started to cry and at that point his parents calmed down and tried to reassure him. Through his sobs, he asked "Daddy, don't you love Mummy anymore?" "Yes, I do, very much", "And Mummy, do you love Daddy?" There was a long pause and then a quiet and simple "Yes". He then returned to his breakfast because as far as he was concerned there was nothing else to talk about: his parents still loved each other but Daddy obviously loves another woman as well. So why were they getting so cross with each other? What was the problem? In his world there wasn't one.

---

[3] Don't get too hung up on the stats here. This was a question I Googled and as always many different 'answers' came up. I chose this one to simply make a point.

19

But in his mother's world there was a big one. Who was right? Learned Convention would say his mother. Nature would say: it is what it is. Either way, the relationship didn't survive…

Let's take a step or two back. I was reading the other day about dating on the internet and the difficulties people are having finding a relationship and just importantly how to make it last. In the article relationship counsellor Val Sampson stated "We're not just looking for a romantic partner, we're looking for a friend, sexual partner, co-parent, and sometimes even a business partner". She's right. Nowadays, we are looking for our partner to tick all the boxes. Is that realistic or even possible? I had a friend who summed up her policy on relationships with the immortal line "If they can't fit in, they can fuck off." Nice. Another friend once said that relationships are all about compromise and give and take. She gives and I take.

Most relationships can't work that way, or at least not for long, and as was discussed in a previous chapter, relationship counsellors will advise that you need to have some shared interests but also to have your own which you can share with others outside the relationship. Makes sense; but only as long as those shared interests are not of a sexual nature or at least that is what Learned Convention will tell us…

In the book 'Sex at Dawn' by Christopher Ryan and Cacilda Jetha, they argue that humans were never meant to evolve to be monogamous, and indeed at the beginning of the human race, everything was shared: food, child rearing, clothing, shelter and, yes, sex. If you fancied some sex or sex in a different way and your 'partner' didn't, well, you just went off and found someone who did. You did it openly and matter of factly. Our brains may not think so, but physically it's natural and how it is in nature. Ah yes, but we're not animals I hear some of you say. Well actually we are, just high functioning ones, and as it happens closely related to the bonobo monkey who mostly enjoy a peaceful, non-hierarchical social structure and have lots of sex with lots of other bonobo monkeys. I sometimes wonder if the two are connected.

It is surely worth considering that if our couple at the beginning of this chapter had accepted that sometimes they have different sexual needs (as they have different social needs), and they were honest and open about it but that they still wanted to create a loving home for each other and their son, then that would be better than splitting up? I'm pretty sure that's what their little boy would have wanted.

CHAPTER 8

Resistance is Futile

So give up, let go and be happy

I was once trying to explain to a yoga teacher friend of mine the difference between effort and resistance. I was saying that if you come across resistance then you should stop forcing it because it will eventually hurt you – either mentally or physically or both. She wasn't convinced. She said that seemed to imply that you should never put yourself out, try to overcome obstacles or strive to better yourself because you're bound to come across resistance in the process - and we can't avoid difficult things just because it might hurt us. She was right of course, but I think we were talking at slightly cross-purposes.

Now, just like my friend, yoga is a big part of my life and one of the things I was told when I first started to practice is to always take your body to 'the edge', but not beyond. So in any particular stretching pose, you will get to a point where it starts to feel a little uncomfortable. At that point push a little bit more and there you will find the edge. And it will feel quite a bit more uncomfortable. Push it further and it will really start to hurt and the body will say to your brain, "go any further fella and something's going to break". As one of the main planks of yoga is to always listen to your body, you'd be very well advised to take heed. So effort, yes, to get to the edge, but when that effort results in resistance stop pushing because as Newton discovered in nature there will simply be a force pushing back – and just as hard.

Like anything in life if you achieve something, there is often a feeling of happiness that goes with it. And with equal inevitability, if you don't achieve it a shed load of unhappiness. This attachment to achievement is a dangerous place to be. (Have a look at Chapter 10 where I talk more about attachments and how they will inevitably make you unhappy). It turns out that often the best way of achieving a more challenging pose in yoga is to relax and breathe into it and simply 'let go': in other words the complete opposite to all this striving and effort. So if you want to go for that pose, go for it; and you may get into it or you may not, but actually so what? Try not to attach your happiness to it, but instead relax and let go and see what happens – it may surprise you.

Anyway, this is what I was trying to get across to my friend and after a few days she sent me an email which far more elegantly and succinctly got to the point:

"I was thinking about what you said about happiness and letting go etc this morning on my dog walk. When I'm on the street, my dog Rosie has to be on a lead. However, she pulls like a mad demented thing. It's VERY annoying. Sometimes I get bored of asking her to heel and I let go of the lead and drape it on her back. It's always at that point that she 'heels' a dream. She sticks to my ankle like glue. I let go and she stays close. Funny."

It is funny as it seems so counter intuitive. She doesn't want Rosie to run away and so she puts her on a lead. She resists like crazy. Let go of the lead and she stays close. Turns out she doesn't want to run off either. It's a parallel we can easily transfer to our relationships.

When things start to get a bit difficult we usually believe that the solution is to work harder at the relationship. Be more attentive, do more things together, talk more. 'More' being the operative word. Doing 'less', relaxing and letting go when the going gets tough (like the yoga pose) is surprisingly difficult to do; and bizarrely can feel quite scary and confusing because you've probably been taking the 'more' approach for years and you feel you're going to lose control if you now abandon it. But that kind of control is an illusion because the more we force the issue and push harder, the more it pushes back - just like Rosie the dog. So we usually end up making things worse.

What to do then? Well, every relationship is different and I'm not saying that the silver bullet of better relationships is to do less, but I would suggest that this option be at least considered more often. The Natural Expression way is all about non-forcing and therefore non-resistance. Finding out who each of you really are in a relationship can take time, patience and guidance. As I have said previously it can be a difficult journey but when you get there, being who you actually are will take no effort at all because by definition it is Natural.

CHAPTER 9

The Only Way Not to get Hurt in Love

Letting go of attachments

In my personal 'journey' around all this, and second only to the whole concept of Natural Expression, is the aspect of attachments - what they are and how we deal with them – that has been the most revelationary and yet hardest to get a handle on. And here's the statement that has caused me all the problems.

"Every attachment you have, whatever it is, will eventually, at some point cause you suffering."

Ergo: the only way not to have suffering in my life is to lose all my attachments. Hmmm, not too sure about all this: I mean I have a *lot* of attachments.

Maybe take a minute or two, and have a think about what your attachments are.

Most of us, when asked the question, tend to come up with things we can touch. They range from the flesh and blood (children, partners, friends, pets etc) to inanimate objects such as our homes, cars and our mobile phone perhaps. So will these, eventually, at some point cause you suffering?

Let's come back to that because first we really need to have a think about how we define suffering. The dictionary definition doesn't really help because it connects suffering with pain. This is not right, at least not in Natural Expression. The essence is this: pain is of the whole body and suffering is of the mind. So if you bang your head that's going to hurt and cause you pain; but if you lose your mind that is suffering. Pain is natural, suffering is not. And *all* your attachments, every last one of them, are of the mind.

So let's go back to our touchy feely list of attachments. Can any one of those, let alone all of them, cause suffering of the mind? I'm afraid so. Of course we are talking degrees here; but sadly our children will somehow one day break our hearts, our partners will at times annoy and frustrate us (and possibly a lot more!), your car will break down and your phone will never work in that curious black spot you have in the kitchen. It's easy to be facetious here, but the only way you're not going to suffer with any of these things is if you don't care about them i.e. you are not attached to them.

But the really challenging aspect to all this is not the attachments we can touch, but the ones that we can't. So for example:

Ambition
Prosperity
Health
Happiness
Wellbeing
Religious Faith
Achievements
Enlightenment
Success
Winning
and the two biggest attachments of them all:

Hope
Love

But, I hear you say, we are told over and over again that hope and love are what life is all about, its very essence no less, for without them there is nothing. But they are undoubtedly attachments and inevitably they will cause you suffering. Love hurts? You bet! And of course realising a hope or a desire will surely make you very happy, but equally very unhappy if you don't. It really is true that both triumphs and disasters are imposters of the mind (with apologies to Rudyard Kipling).

So how do you let go of these attachments, even if you wanted to? By giving up and not caring? Yes, that will work. But are you really not going to care about love? And giving up all hope does sound rather desperate. But that can actually be an enormous release from suffering, a weight off your mind, freedom.

The issue is actually more to do with how we understand the phrases 'not caring' or 'giving up'. They have very negative connotations, but they don't have to because this is to do with not caring about the *attachment* to love and hope and you can do that by living a life of unconditional love and unconditional hope. So it doesn't matter about the result or what happens, you will still love and you will still hope, but you just won't suffer. Living without conditions is actually dead easy, but *thinking* about it can be challenging in the extreme. The next chapter explores this concept further.

But before we leave this one, a friend told me the other day when discussing this whole attachment thing that she was a believer in God, and that belief has never caused her suffering and never will. The words she used were "she was at One with her God". The difference here is that this isn't an attachment. If you are at One, you are homogenous; there is no beginning and no end, no differentiation between subject and object. The sense of self is dissolved. You can have this Oneness with another human being too, if you both let go completely and live your life as your 9-Energy Natural Expression.

Finally, for the vast majority of us suffering is a part of our lives. It's a price we think we have to pay for the happy times. This is wrong as that all comes from the mind and the ego; but just remember your suffering will be as a result of what you are attached to and you will only stop getting hurt in love if you are able to let go of that attachment.

CHAPTER 10

You want Unconditional Love?

Just make sure you read the small print

Ah now, doesn't that sound very cynical? What could be purer or better than giving or receiving unconditional love? Why talk about the small print as if it is some sort of contract? Well it's because the phrase is bandied about quite a lot without many of us really thinking properly what it means. Does that matter? Maybe not, but it might not be a bad thing for us to consider how we define the words 'unconditional' and 'love' in our particular world and how that might compare to the Natural World, the point being that these two worlds are the same.

Let's take the easy one first: unconditional. Now we really don't need the help of a dictionary here, because obviously it means 'without conditions'. But have a think about that for a moment because that's one mighty big commitment in whatever way we use it. Giving something unconditionally means you don't care what the recipient does with it and they don't have to reciprocate or even accept it in the first place. Indeed, they could spit it right back in your face or decide to somehow use it against you. You OK with that? You'd better be, because that's unconditional.

Now what about the meaning of the word 'love'? This is not so easy as it's different for everyone, but sometimes it helps to distinguish between 'love' and 'like'. So in a serious relationship if things are getting tricky, we might say that I'm still in love with you but I just don't like you right now. So once you're in love, you're in love, but you can fall in and out of 'like' all the time!

Of course we have different kinds of love for different people. I will always love my daughter, but I fell out of love with her mother many years ago. You can't control love: you fall in or out without any conscious control or effort. You simply can't make yourself love someone nor can you just switch it off – more's the pity.

'Liking' though is different, you have a choice here don't you? If you want to like someone, you can find lots of reasons to like them: how they look, what they say, what they do and so on and these are exactly the same reasons you can have not to like them. Perhaps, we can say then that 'like' is rational and 'love' is irrational? Maybe, but one thing's for certain, there are a lot of conditions when it comes to liking and none whatsoever when it comes to love. So that's what 'unconditional love' is, right? In that definition, yes, but that's not how the vast majority of us use the term.

So my 'spiritual' friend, after she told me about this wonderful guru she found (see Chapter 1), then turned her attention to unconditional love. She told me that thanks to this guru she had found unconditional love and an example of this was the unconditional love she has for her daughter. "So does your unconditional love stretch to the guy who just served us the drinks?" I asked.

"Of course not, I don't know him!" she replied.

"Oh right," I said, "so…er…it's a condition of this unconditional love to know the person." She thought I was being pedantic and just didn't get it. But you see, if you really do love unconditionally, then, well, you love unconditionally; and that's everything and everyone, which like I said earlier is a hell of a commitment. You can't love your daughter unconditionally, because the condition is she has to be your daughter! See what I mean about the small print?

I don't want to get too bogged down in all this definition stuff, and what people mean or don't mean. That's not the point. The point is that 'unconditional love' – and I mean *no* conditions – would be a wonderful place to be. Imagine, truly loving everything and everyone; and nothing, absolutely nothing; no person, no event, no action, no object in this world can change that. I don't really know how the yogis, or anyone else for that matter, define 'enlightenment', but for me it would be 'unconditional love'. And you don't even have to worry about the small print, because there isn't any.

PART 2

The world of 9-Energy Natural Expression

CHAPTER 1

Before we get started

So if you like, this is the technical end of the book and in this part you will be able to work out your own 9-Energy Natural Expression. It will provide a deep insight into the person you really are and what your Natural State of Being is. It will also enable you to discover the Expressions of those around you and how you connect with them. If you have come straight to this part or skipped some of the chapters in Part 1, I just need to re-emphasise two key points:

1. There is no such thing as a good or bad relationship. Or a good 9-Energy Natural Expression or a bad one. Or that one is better or worse than the other. This is really important to understand, as it is impossible for there to be any judgement or qualification. Remember, this is nature. We can perhaps describe an Expression as 'complex' or 'simple' but that's about as far as it goes and if your relationship works, it works, and that's it.

2. As I said in the first chapter of Part 1, everything I tell you here is a lie. It only becomes true if you can prove it for yourself. It may seem odd to write a book on such a premise, but my task is not to try to convince you of anything: I'm not trying to win an argument here. If people say to me "this is all a load of nonsense", I usually reply saying, "yes, and I too was a complete and total sceptic, but I was simply unable to come up with any rational or scientific explanation for what was going on here. Every time I referred to it, it proved unnervingly accurate nearly all of the time and that cannot be by chance or coincidence, as the maths is simply unable to support that." Some minds may then become open, others will remain

closed; it matters not a jot to me. For the minds that do start to open, it just may be the beginning of a more peaceful and happier life.

The other thing that needs addressing at this point is where does all this stuff come from? The easy answer is from the accumulated observations of Chinese sages going back thousands of years. It is very important to understand that this came first: in other words the sages observed every aspect of the world we live in (humans, animals, plants, minerals, weather etc) and associated their characteristics with 9 Expressions. They didn't come up with this on a whim and then try to shoe-horn people's behaviour into 9 convenient little boxes. If they had, I wouldn't have been drawn to this. So it's not "you're a Fire Expression and therefore you're this, this and this"; but rather a lot of your characteristics and the way you live your life are shared by a particular group of people and they could be likened to the way fire manifests in nature. I liked that and it made a lot of sense to me.

It is, in many ways, a hugely complicated subject open to many different interpretations. Indeed there are people (gurus if you like) who, having studied classical Chinese medicine over many years, may somehow claim that their interpretation is 'definitive'. Some for instance do not differentiate between males and females (although this appears to be more to do with the differences between Japanese and Chinese interpretations), others will use different dating systems and still others will place Wind and Sky Expressions within different Phases (don't worry, all will be explained later).

All of this is simply different interpretations and I refer you to the "everything I tell you is a lie" line above. The fact is there is a huge amount of information out there, printed and online, that goes into enormous detail about how all this works – the 'nuts and bolts' of it all. That's fine but that's not what this book is actually about.

The analogy I think which works well is that it's not unlike a relationship with a car. Yes, we can study how the suspension geometry works and wonder at the inner workings of the internal combustion engine. Or we can simply jump in, take the car out for a spin and just marvel at how well it gets us from A to B! This is the focus of my book. From my own experience and research, I have found a 'car' that I like, customised it a bit here and there to make it work better for me and then offered myself as your driver. It's your choice if you want to come along. Beware though that the journey may be long and difficult, but that's OK because the journey itself is actually every bit as remarkable as the final destination!

CHAPTER 2

What actually is 9-Energy Natural Expression?

Most of us probably know what star sign we are: mine is Libra. A lot of us will also know what creature we are within the Chinese animal zodiac. I'm a rat. The former is based upon a period of the year you were born, the latter on the actual year you were born. Collectively these are aspects of what is called the 12 Branches.

The 9-Energies in effect lie beneath the 12 Branches and your 9-Energy Natural Expression is unique to you and is created from the exact time and place of your birth. In practice though we really only need consider your birth year and month and that is what we will be doing here. Whereas I always struggled with the too broad strokes that the 12 Branches provide, I was blown away by the insight and accuracy of what was revealed by the 9-Energies.

But let's break down what is meant by 9-Energy Natural Expression, and take the last part first: Natural Expression.

Your Natural Expression is how you were as a child of around 3 to 4 years old. Of course it is unlikely that you will remember how you were back then but unless you were the victim of abuse or something similarly vile, you wouldn't have been depressed about what happened in your past or have had any anxiety of what your future would hold. You would have taken people at face value looking past anything to do with race, sex, age or disability. If you liked them, you liked them; and if you didn't you didn't. If you liked someone one day and not the next, it didn't matter a jot because you only judged a person by how you found them there and then. You lived in the present moment, totally honest and natural about the things that were going on for you and what you wanted or didn't want to do. You laughed when you were happy and cried when you were not. Any fear you experienced would have been based on a real or very imminent danger to your well-being. We might call this enlightened state 'mindfulness' or just simply being a child.

However we describe it, this child will be displaying their 9-Energy Natural Expression and only gradually, as they grow older, will this start to be hidden by the burdens of Learned Convention (see Part 1 Chapter 6). When you feel a connection with this philosophy and if you happen to have a child of this sort of age or approaching it, by discovering their 9-Energy Natural Expression you will be able to mitigate both the effects of Learned Convention and your own prejudices and allow your child to express themselves freely. As they grow into adulthood, they will thank you for it!

So what about the 9-Energy part? If you were to research the subject, you may well come across it described as 9 Star Ki. Ki is the Japanese word for Life Force (the Chinese use Chi and the Hindus Prana). The sages believed that Ki energy originated deep in the Cosmos, and this was channelled towards Earth primarily by 9 stars, hence the term 9-Energy. Their observations of nature's phenomena over many centuries gave rise to the cyclical nature of energy in the Universe: in essence that there was a repeating 9 year and 9 month cycle of Ki on Earth which were related to the solar and lunar cycles and which in turn affected people's mental and physical State of Being. The 9 Energies were linked with these cycles and associated with characteristics of the energy in that particular cycle, giving us 9 specific Expressions.

Still with me? Actually it doesn't matter if you're not because all you really need to know is these are the 9 Expressions and you are going be one of them.

1. Sea
2. Earth (as in a field)
3. Thunder
4. Wind
5. Earth Core (as in the centre of the Earth)
6. Sky
7. Lake
8. Mountain
9. Fire

The actual value of the numbers attached to each Expression is not significant as such, but are simply used as a short-hand way of associating an Expression. (So you could say "I'm a Mountain Expression or an 8 Expression", both ways are fine).

Your 9-Energy Natural Expression is actually made up of 3 numbers and is set at the moment you were born. Now depending on what type of calendar you refer to that particular moment can vary. It's easy to get too prescriptive here and that will be a mistake. I use the Chinese calendar to determine the year and the Gregorian calendar for the month and that's because from my experience it provides the most accurate description of your Expression. If you were born on or close to the cusp of the year or month, consider the Expression on either side and go with what feels intuitively and instinctively right for you.

The 3 numbers are made up of the following:

1. Primary or Principal number: this first number is the most significant and influential and is your intrinsic nature. It is derived from the year you were born using the Chinese lunar year starting Feb 4th. (The system I use is related to Chinese Feng Shui (as opposed to the Japanese 9 Star Ki) in that I do differentiate between males and females.
2. Control number: the second number is believed to be associated with your spirituality and driving force. It relates to the solar month you were born using the Gregorian calendar.
3. Energetic or Tendency number: the third number is derived from the combination of the year and the month you were born and can be associated with your habits and typical behaviour.

However, in practical and pragmatic terms, it is perfectly acceptable to use the second and third numbers as a means to qualify your Principal number thereby reinforcing or diminishing its power and influence. Or another way of looking at it is to say the last two numbers are adding shade to the number one base colour.

Using the tables in Chapter 4, you will be able to work out your own 9-Energy Natural Expression but please don't fall into the trap of thinking my 9-Energy Natural Expression is this, therefore I must be that and I will have a good relationship with this person and not with that person. This is because just as we all have Yin and Yang within us, we also have all the 9 Expressions, just in different proportions.

Given the 9 year and 9 month cycles and the associated Expressions, there are 81 different 9-Energy Natural Expressions and there is an interpretation or reading of each one of them in Chapter 5. But before then, we need to explore Yin and Yang a little further and also some of the other phenomena which influence the makeup of your Natural Expression. It might all seem pretty complicated (and actually it is!) but if you're not really that interested or bothered about how the interpretations are arrived at, you won't miss out on anything if you skip the next chapter!

CHAPTER 3

How Yin and Yang, 5 phases, 5 elements, 4 seasons and the 9 family members all fit in

If you've come with me from the previous chapter, the title of this one describes some of the other phenomena which are considered when interpreting your 9-Energy Natural Expression. All play their part, but none more so than the forces of Yin and Yang. But before we get to that, let's have a closer look at the source of all this: the incredible and truly awesome book that is the I Ching.

I Ching

As I mentioned in the first part of the book the foundations of this whole philosophy can be found in the I Ching or Book of Changes. Said to have been written 5000 years ago by the Chinese Emperor Fu Xi, this ancient book still provides us with many valuable philosophical and ethical truths. It's as relevant today as it was back then because the fundamentals of nature and humanity do not and indeed cannot change. It can be easy to dismiss this book as the stuff of mystics, fortune tellers and sensible people who should know better, but Western science, specifically within the fields of quantum physics, biophysics, neuroscience and bioenergetics do acknowledge the wisdom and universal laws that are found in Eastern philosophies generally and the I Ching in particular.

There are many people who have acknowledged how influential the I Ching was in their lives, Apple founder Steve Jobs being a case in point. But I was particularly taken by the years of study devoted to the I Ching by the psychoanalyst Carl Jung, who based his Theory of Synchronicity on it; as well as Wolfgang Pauli, the Nobel Prize winning quantum physicist, who collaborated with Jung to discover it gave insight into the binary nature of the universe. And Bob Dylan, a spokesman for a generation, was quoted as saying "I don't have any religion or philosophy, I can't say much about them, but there is a book called the I Ching, I'm not trying to push it, I don't want to talk about it, but it's the only thing that is amazingly true, period..."

So now let's turn to what the I Ching said about the forces of Yin and Yang.

Yin and Yang

The I Ching included an explanation of the fundamental laws of humanity and showed that everything that happens in our lives, indeed in the whole universe, is the result of two equal but opposite interacting forces called Yin and Yang. With nothing being wholly Yin or wholly Yang, their relationship to each other is one of constant change: uniting, transforming, separating and regenerating. Yin is said to be feminine, yielding, fertile and of the Earth; whilst Yang is masculine, masterful, creative and of the Heavens. Yin is the core and it's like a beehive. At the centre is the queen bee, the ultimate expression of Yin, which is vulnerable and needs protecting and that's the job of the worker bees, the Yang expression, which fly around the hive guarding the queen. Both need the other. It can be fun to imagine if the roles of the king and queen were reversed in a game of chess with the Yang king now being able to move where it likes and in any direction, and he and all the rest of the pieces are there to protect the Yin queen. Now that would reflect the YinYang world of nature, for if the Yin queen falls, the game is lost...

We can also associate the following opposites with Yin and Yang:

Yin	Yang
Maternal	Paternal
Introvert	Extrovert
Accumulating	Expanding
Flexible	Stubborn
Soft	Hard
Dependent	Independent

Yin	Yang
Cool	Passionate
Chronic	Acute
Stillness	Movement
Cold	Hot
Cautious	Bold
Slow	Fast
Deep	Superficial
Quiet	Loud
Diligent	Impulsive
Grief, fearful, unclear	Anger, excitability, anxiety
Sensitive	Insensitive

By way of summary the following four primary principles explain the relationship between Yin and Yang:

1. All phenomena contain two inherent but opposing forces
2. Yin and Yang depend upon each other
3. Yin and Yang nurture each other
4. Between Yin and Yang there is a transformative potential.

We can illustrate these principles using the traditional YinYang symbol:

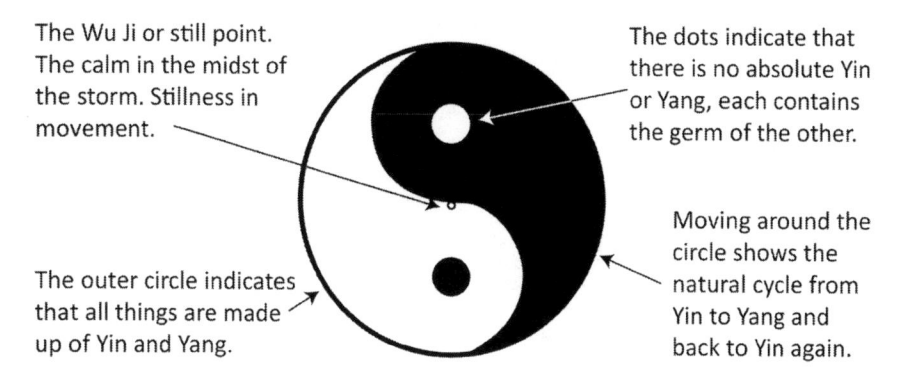

The Wu Ji or still point. The calm in the midst of the storm. Stillness in movement.

The dots indicate that there is no absolute Yin or Yang, each contains the germ of the other.

The outer circle indicates that all things are made up of Yin and Yang.

Moving around the circle shows the natural cycle from Yin to Yang and back to Yin again.

So with everything in the universe being made up of Yin and Yang to varying proportions, it follows that the 9 Expressions adhere to the same principle but proportionally speaking 3 Thunder is the most Yang and 7 Lake is the most Yin.

This is the order:

$$\left.\begin{array}{l}3 \text{ Thunder} \\ 6 \text{ Sky} \\ 5 \text{ Earth Core} \\ 8 \text{ Mountain} \\ 1 \text{ Sea}\end{array}\right\} \text{Yang}$$

$$\left.\begin{array}{l}9 \text{ Fire} \\ 4 \text{ Wind} \\ 2 \text{ Earth} \\ 7 \text{ Lake}\end{array}\right\} \text{Yin}$$

Now it's time to see how the 9 Expressions fit into what is known as the 5 Transformative Phases and how that gives us the 5 Elements: this is the basis of what guides and provides insight into the nature and dynamics of our relationships.

5 Phases, 5 Elements and 4 Seasons

So with Yin and Yang laying the foundations, it was further observed by those wise sages back then that all things in nature have 5 specific transformative phases within their birth-to-death life cycle namely: Creation – Gestation – Consolidation – Maturation – Dissolution, and these can be illustrated like so:

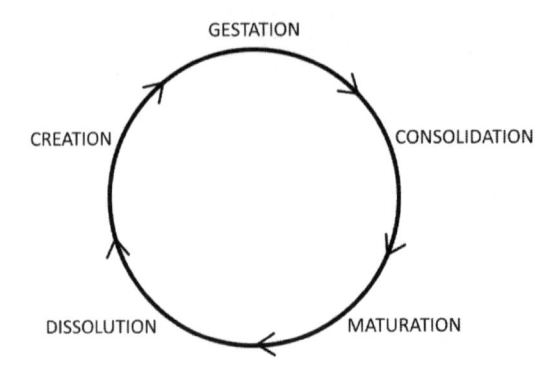

```
              GESTATION
         ╱─────────────╲
   CREATION           CONSOLIDATION
         ╲─────────────╱
      DISSOLUTION   MATURATION
```

Sex, Love and Who Puts the Rubbish Out?

Each of these 5 phases was eventually given a name or metaphors designated to different Elements to describe their properties. They were also related to a time of the day and a particular season of the year. The Elements assigned to the different phases in the birth-to-death cycle are described below and each of the 9 Expressions will belong in one of these 5 phases:

1. **Wood (Creation)**, not dead wood, but alive like a tree; it therefore symbolises all living things. It represents birth, like a tree breaking through the ground for the first time and the beginning of the life cycle. It's associated with the dawn and spring season and windy and changeable weather. Those born within this phase tend to have plenty of ideas and initial energy and enthusiasm but can sometimes lack the stamina and focus to see the task through. The Expressions 3 Thunder and 4 Wind are in the Wood phase.

2. **Fire (Gestation)** is like the blossoming of life, expansive and vibrant, and outwardly the most active of the elements. It represents midday and the height of summer. People with Fire in their 9-Energy Natural Expression tend to be passionate, expressive, warm and sociable. It is associated with success, but also pride which if allowed to develop into hubris can lead to a fall. Only the 9 Fire Expression is in the Fire phase.

3. **Earth (Consolidation)**, as in the soil, not the planet. It symbolises the start of consolidation and settling down after the Fire. Its nature is grounding and downward and associated with the afternoon and the late summer/early autumn when the weather is damp or humid. These people tend to be grounded, practical, supportive and nurturing. They have the power to control those around them and will accomplish their goals through effort and dedication. It is the element of accumulation: belongings, wealth, emotions – and sometimes grudges! Three Expressions: 2 Earth, 5 Earth Core and 8 Mountain sit in the Earth phase.

4. **Metal (Maturation)** is further consolidation and symbolises maturity and stability. It represents the harvest and the first chilly evenings of autumn. People with this element can stand confidently on their own and be clear and decisive in their decisions and

actions: they can have a natural sense of authority, but sometimes can be too inward looking. 6 Sky and 7 Lake are in the Metal phase.

5. **Water (Dissolution)**, whilst representing the end of the life cycle, it is also where things go into hibernation preparing for new life to emerge in the coming spring. It is of the cold winter nights. These types can be deep and reflective and are often very independent but can be very insecure too, which they are often successful at hiding. Just the 1 Sea is in the Water phase.

By way of summary:

Phase	Creation	Gestation	Consolidation	Maturation	Dissolution
Element	Wood	Fire	Earth	Metal	Water
Time of Day	Dawn	Noon	Afternoon	Evening	Night
Season	Spring	Summer	Early Autumn	Late Autumn	Winter
Expression	3 Tree 4 Wind	9 Fire	2 Earth 5 Earth Core 8 Mountain	6 Sky 7 Lake	1 Sea
General Characteristics	Creative Initially energetic Lacks stamina	Passionate Expressive Hubristic	Practical Accumulating Controlling	Confident Authoritative Introspective	Independent Deep Insecure

It's how these Phases, Elements, Expressions and their YinYang forces interact with each other that provide the remarkable insight into our relationships. This will be looked at closely in Chapter 6 of this part of the book and also where we get to study something called the 5 Transformation Diagram which shows in detail how all these forces relate to each other. Here's a sneak preview (and don't worry about the internal arrows, all will be revealed later!):

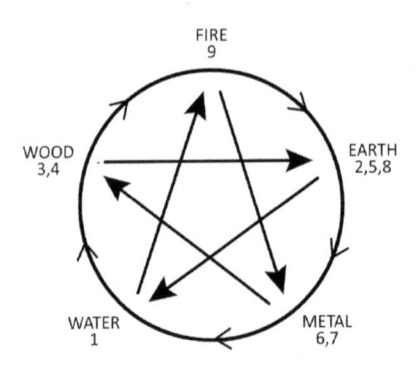

Sex, Love and Who Puts the Rubbish Out?

Before we finish this chapter, we need to have a look at how the I Ching describes the hierarchy of the family and how that adds another layer to your Expression.

9 Family Members

OK, in actual fact, the I Ching only describes 8 family members: father, mother, eldest son, eldest daughter, middle son, middle daughter, youngest son and youngest daughter. So where does the ninth family member fit in? Well, he or she fits in the middle or centre of the family and is described by some as the Seventh Child.

Each of the Expressions is equated to a particular member of the family and even though there is a gender attached to them, it is not to be taken literally but rather as their quality or characteristic as the 'Father' for instance can be male or female.

Father (6 Sky)

This is the archetypal male quality, so these people (remember can be male or female) tend to be straightforward and practical. They have a natural air of authority and often take the leadership role within the family, local communities and the workplace. They strive for fairness but in doing so can sometimes appear too inflexible and not fully taking into account the situation facing them.

Mother (2 Earth)

This is the archetypical female quality. Like the father they try to provide a fair environment but will bring their more feminine characteristics to bear such as caring, supportiveness, empathy and diplomacy. Whilst like the father they can take on a leadership role, they tend to work better in groups where they are more inclusive and open in how they deal with the people around them.

Eldest Son (3 Thunder)

The first-born is the trailblazer: exploring and trying new things and being allowed to make mistakes along the way, although that can sometimes mean they are rash and impulsive. They lay the path for their siblings, both in how they lead their life and the examples they set.

Eldest Daughter (4 Wind)

Similar to the eldest son, these types are creative and imaginative and want to explore new ways to express themselves both personally and professionally, and can therefore be seen as rebellious and non-conformist. They can both influence and be influenced by people and situations, sometimes leading to indecision.

Middle Son (1 Sea)

Sitting between the eldest and the youngest, these people tend to be easy going and good at resolving heated conflicts and arguments. Using their soft and thoughtful manner, they will listen to both sides and present solutions that go a long way to satisfying everyone.

Middle Daughter (9 Fire)

Like the middle son, they too will attempt to resolve conflicts but rather than taking time to consider all the arguments, they will often come to a conclusion quickly shedding light on the issue and making it 'obvious' what the right course of action should be. They tend to be highly active and outgoing with a direct approach that can be both challenging and dazzling.

Youngest Son (8 Mountain)

As the youngest member of the family, they have seen and learnt from the experiences of their parents and older siblings and therefore tend to be reflective in their outlook. They are usually deep thinkers, quiet and highly intelligent. Adventurous and self-reliant they can sometimes be a little too introspective.

Youngest Daughter (7 Lake)

Similar to the youngest son, these people bring a wealth of experience to their outlook on life. Reflective and generally optimistic, they can be very sentimental and sometimes pretty emotional and tend to be more open to a spiritual way of life.

Seventh Child (5 Earth Core)

These people are usually at the centre of things and in touch and relate well with all the other members of the family, although that doesn't stop them acting independently of them. Very strong personalities, they can control situations well, have the ability to lead and like to get involved in new projects and ideas.

And just before we go...

I know many of you will just want to discover what your 9-Energy Natural Expression is and what that means for you and your relationships (the next few chapters will satisfy that!). But just before we leave this one, it is worth emphasising the enormous power and insight that the I Ching has brought to humanity. To explore, explain and rationalise the cycles, balances and inter-connectedness of all of nature thousands of years before Western science had a go is really quite remarkable. Now that Western science has backed most of it up, even more so perhaps given the scepticism that the modern world tends to have of the ancient, so called mystical world. But enough; now to the tables and insights into the world of 9-Energy Natural Expression!

CHAPTER 4

Working out your 9-Energy Natural Expression

Your 9-Energy Natural Expression is actually made up by a combination of 3 Expressions; but rather than using the actual name of the Expression, it is typical (and easier) if they are referred to by their associated number. (Chapter 2 in this part of the book explains all this in more detail).

The most important number is your Primary Number and that depends upon the year you were born, commencing on the 4th of February. So if you were born between the 1st January and the 3rd February, you will fall into the previous calendar year. Your first two numbers are also gender specific.

Primary Number

\multicolumn{9}{c	}{MALES}
9 Fire Yin	8 Mountain Yang	7 Lake Yin	6 Sky Yang	5 Earth Core Yang	4 Wind Yin	3 Thunder Yang	2 Earth Yin	1 Sea Yang
1910	1911	1912	1913	1914	1915	1916	1917	1918
1919	1920	1921	1922	1923	1924	1925	1926	1927
1928	1929	1930	1931	1932	1933	1934	1935	1936
1937	1938	1939	1940	1941	1942	1943	1944	1945
1946	1947	1948	1949	1950	1951	1952	1953	1954
1955	1956	1957	1958	1959	1960	1961	1962	1963
1964	1965	1966	1967	1968	1969	1970	1971	1972
1973	1974	1975	1976	1977	1978	1979	1980	1981
1982	1983	1984	1985	1986	1987	1988	1989	1990
1991	1992	1993	1994	1995	1996	1997	1998	1999
2000	2001	2002	2003	2004	2005	2006	2007	2008
2009	2010	2011	2012	2013	2014	2015	2016	2017
2018	2019	2020	2021	2022	2023	2024	2025	2026

Rick Nunn

FEMALES								
6 Sky Yang	7 Lake Yin	8 Mountain Yang	9 Fire Yin	1 Sea Yang	2 Earth Yin	3 Thunder Yang	4 Wind Yin	5 Earth Core Yang
1910	1911	1912	1913	1914	1915	1916	1917	1918
1919	1920	1921	1922	1923	1924	1925	1926	1927
1928	1929	1930	1931	1932	1933	1934	1935	1936
1937	1938	1939	1940	1941	1942	1943	1944	1945
1946	1947	1948	1949	1950	1951	1952	1953	1954
1955	1956	1957	1958	1959	1960	1961	1962	1963
1964	1965	1966	1967	1968	1969	1970	1971	1972
1973	1974	1975	1976	1977	1978	1979	1980	1981
1982	1983	1984	1985	1986	1987	1988	1989	1990
1991	1992	1993	1994	1995	1996	1997	1998	1999
2000	2001	2002	2003	2004	2005	2006	2007	2008
2009	2010	2011	2012	2013	2014	2015	2016	2017
2018	2019	2020	2021	2022	2023	2024	2025	2026

Second Number

Once you know your Primary number, you can work out your Second number from the month you were born starting from the first day of that month.

MALES			
Primary	1,4,7	3,6,9	2,5,8
February	8	5	2
March	7	4	1
April	6	3	9
May	5	2	8
June	4	1	7
July	3	9	6
August	2	8	5
September	1	7	4
October	9	6	3
November	8	5	2
December	7	4	1
January	6	3	9

FEMALES			
Primary	1,4,7	3,6,9	2,5,8
February	7	1	4
March	8	2	5
April	9	3	6
May	1	4	7
June	2	5	8
July	3	6	9
August	4	7	1
September	5	8	2
October	6	9	3
November	7	1	4
December	8	2	5
January	9	3	6

Sex, Love and Who Puts the Rubbish Out?

Third Number

Your third number is worked out with your Primary number and your Second number using the table below. Put all 3 numbers together and that is your 9-Energy Natural Expression.

Primary / Second	1	2	3	4	5	6	7	8	9
1	1-1-5	2-1-6	3-1-7	4-1-8	5-1-9	6-1-1	7-1-2	8-1-3	9-1-4
2	1-2-4	2-2-5	3-2-6	4-2-7	5-2-8	6-2-9	7-2-1	8-2-2	9-2-3
3	1-3-3	2-3-4	3-3-5	4-3-6	5-3-7	6-3-8	7-3-9	8-3-1	9-3-2
4	1-4-2	2-4-3	3-4-4	4-4-5	5-4-6	6-4-7	7-4-8	8-4-9	9-4-1
5	1-5-1	2-5-2	3-5-3	4-5-4	5-5-5	6-5-6	7-5-7	8-5-8	9-5-9
6	1-6-9	2-6-1	3-6-2	4-6-3	5-6-4	6-6-5	7-6-6	8-6-7	9-6-8
7	1-7-8	2-7-9	3-7-1	4-7-2	5-7-3	6-7-4	7-7-5	8-7-6	9-7-7
8	1-8-7	2-8-8	3-8-9	4-8-1	5-8-2	6-8-3	7-8-4	8-8-5	9-8-6
9	1-9-6	2-9-7	3-9-8	4-9-9	5-9-1	6-9-2	7-9-3	8-9-4	9-9-5

Here are some 9-Enegy Natural Expressions for some famous people:

Politics	Date of Birth	9-Energy Natural Expression
Tony Blair	6th May 1953	2-8-8
David Cameron	9th October 1966	7-9-3
Hilary Clinton	26th October 1947	7-6-6
Barak Obama	4th August 1961	3-8-9
Ronald Reagan	6th February 1911	8-2-2
Margaret Thatcher	13th October 1925	3-9-8
Donald Trump	14th June 1946	9-1-4
Sport		
Muhammad Ali	17th January 1942	5-9-1
David Beckham	2nd May 1975	7-5-7
Jessica Ennis-Hill	28th January 1986	9-3-2
Lewis Hamilton	7th January 1985	7-6-6
Serena Williams	26th September 1981	5-2-8
Tiger Woods	30th December 1975	7-7-5

Music		
Adele	5th May 1988	3-4-4
Beyonce	4th September 1981	5-2-8
Ice Cube	15th June 1969	4-4-5
Lady Gaga	28th March 1986	1-8-7
John Lennon	9th October 1940	6-6-5
Madonna	16th August 1958	9-7-7
Paul McCartney	18th June 1942	4-4-5
Harry Styles	1st February 1994	7-8-4
Actors/Celebrity		
Jennifer Lawrence	15th August 1990	5-1-9
Simon Cowell	7th October 1959	5-3-7
Lea Seydoux	1st July 1985	9-6-8
Tom Hanks	9th July 1956	8-6-7
Kim Kardashian	21st October 1980	4-6-3
Will Smith	25th September 1968	5-4-6
Oprah Winfrey	29th January 1954	4-9-9
Business		
Richard Branson	18th July 1950	5-6-4
Bill Gates	28th October 1950	9-6-8
Steve Jobs	24th February 1955	9-5-8
Mark Zuckerberg	14th May 1984	7-5-7

You might want to make a note of some of the people in your life and their 9-Energy Natural Expressions.

Romantic	Date of Birth	9-Energy Natural Expression

Personal		
Professional		

The next chapter now goes into the details: firstly summarising the key features of each Expression, the kind of person you are and the type of relationship you will have with your own and other Expressions (chapter 6 explains the different types of relationships you can have). It then goes on to describe your general characteristics and how that manifests within males and females and what that means in matters of sex and love. Finally, each of the 81 9-Energy Natural Expressions are given their own specific profile.

CHAPTER 5
Revealing your 9-Energy Natural Expression

Sea Expressions

Number: 1
Phase: Water
Season: Winter

Force: Yang
Family Member: Middle Son
Time of day: Night

What kind of person you are:
* Cool * Independent * Concentrating * Intuitive * Diplomatic * Serious * Careful * Insightful * Obstinate * Tenacious * Worrisome * Social * Self-Protective * Industrious * Insecure * Patient * Hardworking * Intimate * Self-Assertive * Manipulative

Relationships: 1 with 1: Friendship (Yang/Yang)
1 with 2: Passive Control (Yang/Yin)
1 with 3: Parent-Child (Yang/Yang)
1 with 4: Parent-Child (Yang/Yin)
1 with 5: Conflict Opposites (Yang/Yang)
1 with 6: Child-Parent (Yang/Yang)
1 with 7: Child-Parent (Yang/Yin)
1 with 8: Conflict Opposites (Yang/Yang)
1 with 9: Compatible Opposites (Yang/Yin)

Generally Speaking

There tends to be two sides to Sea Expressions: gloomy and somewhat negative or lively and positive, the latter being most apparent in dark or difficult times. Your relationship with your parents (especially the father) can be distant and your childhood may have been fraught with difficulty but this gives you a patient and independent nature creating the ingredients for future success.

Fiercely independent, deep-thinking loners, you are both intelligent and talented and resist strongly being pushed around or confined by people or situations. You'll play to your own tune and whilst you are fairly intense and taciturn by nature, you can be blunt and to the point when you do speak out especially when seeking the truth and justice.

There is a domineering and insensitive side to you and a marked stubborn streak but you are strong and dependable when the going gets tough and really good at cooling hotheads and calming angry confrontations with your sound and rational arguments. You need and like being challenged but your sense of independence can cause difficulties as it can lead to over-confidence and then to loneliness and isolation.

Whilst you can have difficulties finishing things, you can take up a leadership position comfortably and relate well to strangers (often better than your own family and relatives), which allows you to develop a wide circle of friends and associates, although few will get to know you deep down as you will keep your true emotions and feelings secret. That being said, there may be a deep sense of mystery and darkness to you, but of all the Expressions yours is the inner light that is the most pure and true.

Males:

Sea is a Yang Expression and this suits the male body well but the combination can make men of this type cold and arrogant and if taken to extremes you will become social outcasts. You nearly always see the negative before the positive but more than most will delve deeply into areas where others fear to go on issues such as sex, corruption and conspiracies for example. Tough and to the point, you constantly seek the truth and have a strict code of honesty which others can find hard to follow.

Because of this natural tendency to go into the depth of things, you accumulate vast oceans of knowledge and often become prominent thinkers and intellectuals as a result. It could lead you down the path to investigative journalism or detective work but this can take you to the dark and murky depths which will leave a deep impression on your moral outlook.

You can be very secretive and will often only share what you know with people you trust and whilst you can come across as hard and critical and rather aloof, there is an inner fire which can shine brightly and warmly and inspire those around you.

Females:

It is the power of the sea that makes this Yang Expression complex for the female but the results are usually strong women who instinctively take on leadership roles both within the family and in business; not only in the general direction of things but also with the finances. It can lead you though into messy and confrontational situations as you can be narrow-minded and unwilling to take on other people's views and opinions.

Similar to male Sea Expressions, you will leave no stone unturned to seek out the truth especially in matters of philosophy and the heart, where your intense thinking and deep knowledge leads to you poetry, music and acting allowing you to express your strong emotions.

As with 7 Lake Expressions, even though you may appear cool and powerful on the outside, you have a warm heart but you can be quite negative in your outlook, to the point and pushy even. However more than most, you can get through hard and difficult times where your focus and independent mind-set puts you at an advantage.

You tend to feel more comfortable in the company of Yang and Yin males and to an extent Yang females rather than Yin females; but partnership wise, it is the Yin male that provides the balance as long as the male is secure and understands your need for independence and time on your own. It follows then that as mothers you tend to better understand your Yang children as they will seek their independence more quickly.

Sex:

This is a very powerful Expression when it comes to sex – one of the most passionate of all the Expressions. But in keeping with the two sides of Sea, you can either be shy, indecisive and cautious when it comes to sex leading to long periods of celibacy especially if your advances have been rejected; or your very strong sexual feelings come surging to the surface in an adventurous and almost animalistic way which can either be expressed with many partners in different situations or in a very deep and spiritual way in a secure one-to-one relationship.

Love:

These Expressions like to have companionship and your love for your partner will run deep and powerful but you need to have your solitude too. For you these two states are not incompatible and partners to Sea Expressions need to understand that they may be 'with' you, but not actually a part of you. This may feel dispiriting but Sea Expressions consider deeply when choosing their partners and once committed are loyal and loving. This could actually lead to you being clingy or over lavish when it comes to praise or gifts especially if you feel you are about to be dumped. As the Middle Son, you are natural listeners and communicators and you must surrender to this in order to maintain and enhance closeness with your partner otherwise your bias towards solitude could leave you isolated and lonely.

9-Energy Natural Expressions:

1-1-5:

This is a triple Yang Natural Expression, which sits comfortably for a man but not so much for a woman. The 5 in your Expression means that you're going to be found at the centre of things such as family, local community and at work. You're going to have firm ideas about how things should be done and are likely to be very independent, detail-conscious, bright and adventurous with a deep philosophical nature. You can be quite secretive and often struggle to understand other people's problems and can even be quite dismissive, but there is a large capacity for cool judgement, pragmatism and real warmth. You need to seek Yin Expressions for balance.

1-2-4:

The two Yin Expressions (2 and 4) will temper the 1 Yang; so whilst there is still that independent, serious and stubborn streak, there is also a warm and easy-going side that enjoys social occasions and mixing with people you know and are comfortable with. There is definitely a strong, steady driving force in this Expression especially if it is directed towards human rights, justice and fairness. You can appear to be quite conservative and quiet but this is just as likely to be hiding a thirst for adventure and trying new things. There are balances to be found in this Expression and generally it sits well for both males and females.

1-3-3:

A triple Yang Expression, you have an underlying nature to control and impose yourself on others. You can be very self-assertive, direct and to the point. For men, this might be seen as typical 'alpha male' behaviour; for women it is a complex Expression and you may feel the need to 'tone down' your assertiveness although to do that for any length of time would be wrong and will cause you suffering and illness. In any case, just under the surface there is a very sensitive side which gets easily hurt if those around you can't see that. You are hardworking (which can lead to obsessiveness), impatient but caring and tend to have a strong sex drive. You need to listen and be influenced by Yin Expressions to provide balance and calming.

1-4-2:

From the outside, this Expression may appear quiet, reliable, tender and sometimes moody. But this hides a strong, self-assertive and independent individual with a strong sense of adventure. However, there is a rather emotional side to you coupled with a conservative and stubborn streak. Intelligent and helpful, you can be self-centred, somewhat opinionated and difficult for others to read. The maternal instinct is strong for the females but you will want to do more than simply staying at home. In the work environment, this Expression is characterised by being steady, dependable and loyal. Given the choice, you are likely to want to remain in one place for a good length of time.

1-5-1:

You are likely to come across as quite shy and serious. You are independent, ambitious, flexible and creative, but underneath there is a strong sense of worry and insecurity. To counter this, you will frequently seek the attention and approval of others and meticulously and patiently make plans for the future. There is a lot of strength to see things through but it's just that you struggle to do it totally independently. You can be bold and quite demanding in your relationships and have a strong sexual desire. This undercurrent of insecurity and dependency means that you are uncomfortable cutting off all relations with ex-partners and you will find your best fit with secure and undemanding Yin Expressions.

1-6-9:

The 9 Fire in this Expression gives these people a charismatic and flamboyant exterior and you like being at the centre of things. Your social circle tends to be small however, as you have trouble compromising and have clear demarcation lines between those who are 'with you' and those 'against you'. There is a strong sense of pride with this Expression and you take badly to being criticised. You tend to live your life through intuition and instincts and can struggle to communicate and explain your thoughts and motives. Independent and impatient, both men and women can sometimes find settling into relationships and family life difficult.

1-7-8:

You are hardworking, self-assertive and independent. You are also self-conscious and very sensitive. This can make you appear quiet and rather negative but in actual fact there is much strength and energy at the core of this Expression. At work and in your life generally, you are methodical, direct and detail conscious with a great ability to focus on the matter at hand. You are apt to make definitive decisions which can give you great angst if you spend time reflecting on it. Naturally family orientated, you have a fun and playful side which those close to you will see and love and you have the knack of making people feel welcome and at ease.

1-8-7:

Ambitious and hardworking, this Expression comes across as sociable, fun and easy-going but with a strong sense of independence. You do need to have time by yourself and will retreat into your 'cave' and whilst there you are likely to be uncommunicative and withdrawn but it is just your way of dealing with life and controlling your sensitive nature. You are easily upset and hate to lose face and so can struggle making decisions. You will look to your partner to help you in this regard as well as them organising your life, just as long as it's exactly how you want it to be! It's a sort of independent dependency!

1-9-6:

You like to lead and as a rule you are very good at it! This is because you can combine your natural charisma and creativity with prudence and directness. You make persuasive and convincing speakers although with a tendency to 'guild the lily'. You can be moody and make snap, thoughtless judgements or labour making decisions to a point of virtual paralysis. You can be rather self-centred and vain but you are a true romantic with great reserves of affection which can truly inspire those around you. You tend to be drawn to well-organised partners who are less self-assertive than you as you are going to be doing the majority of the leading.

Earth Expressions

Number: 2
Phase: Earth
Season: Late Summer/Early Autumn

Force: Yin
Family Member: Mother
Time of Day: Afternoon

What kind of person you are:
* Steady * Stable * Dependent * Sacrificing * Nurturing * Diligent * Patient * Conservative * Gentle * Shrewd * Observant * Detail-minded * Fastidious * Supportive * Methodical * Mothering * Serving * Embracing * Devoted

Relationships: 2 with 1: Passive Control (Yin/Yang)
2 with 2: Friendship (Yin/Yin)
2 with 3: Compatible Opposites (Yin/Yang)
2 with 4: Passive Inertia (Yin/Yin)
2 with 5: Friendship (Yin/Yang)
2 with 6: Parent-Child (Yin/Yang)
2 with 7: Parent-Child (Yin/Yin)
2 with 8: Friendship (Yin/Yang)
2 with 9: Child-Parent (Yin/Yin)

Generally Speaking

The 2 Earth Expression is symbolised by the Mother (as opposed to 6 Sky Expression which is the Father) and is the embodiment of pure and ultimate Yin. Consequently you must seek Yang outside of yourself which can leave you vulnerable to abuse by the Yang. You are definitely people of action, but behind the scenes not in the limelight. You often have a simple and conservative outlook on life which you can stubbornly adhere to, but like the archetypal Mother, you are warm, supportive, devoted and self-sacrificial.

Often slow to adapt to changing circumstances, you need to take things step-by-step but some are desperate to lead and take control too soon and this will be a mistake, as you are more suited to learning from a strong Yang type leader before you take on bigger responsibilities. You are repelled by harsh and abrasive people and can easily fall into a victim state of mind, feeling weak and needy.

There is real depth and solidity to your nature and whilst you are unlikely to be described as an intellectual, you are great at communicating and understanding languages both as a foreign tongue and in scientific terminology. You hate things being over-complicated and can find it hard to concentrate on one thing at a time and instead will try to keep many balls up in the air at the same time often with mixed results.

You really enjoy your social life especially if it revolves around the family and the dining table. Cooking is important to you but primarily as a means to provide nourishment rather than to show-off your culinary skills. You tend to be drawn to the caring professions such as nursing and childcare or to some form of public service such as the police, military or politics.

Males:

Because of the nature of this pure Yin force, it can make it a difficult or 'complex' Expression for males. This is because you can struggle to feel 'masculine' or what Learned Convention tells us should be masculine. As a result, you can go to great lengths to hide these feelings usually by overcompensating in masculine behaviour whilst at the same time not accepting and embracing the female side of your natural softness and this will cause suffering and be unhealthy for you.

You tend to be steady, logical and process-driven and more physical with your bodies than intellectual with your minds. Sociable and popular, you are naturally accommodating, putting yourself out for others and are good at nurturing projects and plans helping them to grow and blossom. Caring professions suit you well such as nursing or charity work particularly with children or the disabled. You also make effective non-divisive politicians or diplomats where your smooth and easy-going demeanour will help break down barriers. Often though, you will end up in traditional 'masculine' professions believing this will hide your Yin tendencies.

It is your caring, patient and maternal nature that draws women towards you as you seem to make the perfect father. The Yang women in your life will dress you well making you look good, although in truth you are really not that bothered! In the bedroom department though there may be difficulties, but only because if you always try to take control and be dominant (believing this is what the man should do), it will be unnatural and unsustainable causing you both unhappiness. You need to accept your Yin, let go and relax and understand that being dependant and being led by Yang (but not being abused) is the way of things and how it has to be.

Females:

For females this is literally the Earth Mother Expression - Yin in its purest form. It is gentle, calm and tolerant, dependable, down-to-earth, patient and supportive. In return, you need love, kindness and attention and of all the Expressions want nothing more than to create life and contentedly nurture your children and feed the family.

It's unnatural for you to force things or be 'showy' although sadly you may think you should be that way to be more 'successful' in today's society. You will know instinctively when things need to change but you will do it gradually in a steady, measured sort of way trying hard not to upset anyone or create waves on the way.

Like all the Expressions in the Earth Phase (2,5,8), you like to collect and hoard things although their value or usefulness is of less importance. However when it comes to finances, you are frugal and excellent at keeping track of your money and keeping accounts. This can sometimes make you appear greedy and selfish but this is unlikely to be directed towards an individual or be anything more sinister than you 'just can't help yourself', as it is simply in your nature to gather and accumulate.

Inevitably, you are attracted to powerful Yang men (the archetypal alpha male) and whilst those kinds of men need your gentleness and softness, they often misunderstand you which can lead to them being forceful and sometimes abusive. You love to be touched and caressed and crave sexual connection but you can find yourself at the beck and call of men and being taken for granted which leaves you hurt and confused or worse bitter and resentful. In response, and without dealing directly with the matter, you might withdraw sex and physical contact coming across as sneaky and manipulative.

You are a 'people person' suiting supportive jobs such as Human Resources, nursing and the caring professions. Your diplomatic and easy social skills make you loved by many around you but you can be plagued by self-doubt and insecurity, convinced you are not good enough and your self-worth can be badly affected.

Sex:

As a rule, 2 Earth Expressions may come across as more reserved when it comes to matters of a sexual nature. That's not to say that sex is unimportant to you but you see it as just one of the many ways to care and show love for your partner. You want to please and this may manifest in a number of ways, but you may supress your own sexual needs or come across as being too easy and available or being the dutiful sexual partner at the beck and call of the more dominant usually Yang partner. If you feel taken for granted for too long, you will feel used, even abused, and this will lead to much unhappiness.

Love:

2 Earth Expressions are the Mother at the family table and so it is unsurprising that motherly qualities are directed towards your partners such as care, love, patience and affection. It is because of these traits that women are attracted to these types of men, whilst the woman is drawn to strong, powerful men. You can suffocate your partners by being obsessive and trying to please too much and being too attentive; or conversely if you feel you are not being seen or heard, trying to be the opposite by displaying passive aggressive tendencies. But generally you are devoted and faithful, happily offering your love without question.

9-Energy Natural Expressions:

2-1-6:

You are bright, sincere, straightforward, organised and logical. You work in a careful, methodical way which can end up being inflexible and bordering on the finicky as you expect things to be perfect. Your focus and steady hard work will provide the recognition you aspire to but don't be afraid to ask for help and support from a stronger Expression to help you get there. For men, you are a lot more serious and sensitive than you let on whilst women like to control and can be obstinate and haughty. You like to help people and to serve but under pressure you can show a tactful and diplomatic side to your character although your decision making might be slow, cautious and over-complicated.

Sex, Love and Who Puts the Rubbish Out?

2-2-5:

You like to be involved and in the middle of things and be appreciated for your efforts. You are steady, supportive, diplomatic and rather conventional. You have a perceptive nature but can be hyper-critical with yourself and those around you and your focus on details can border on fastidious. Your actions tend be deliberate and sometimes over cautious but clear and precise and underlined with a great deal of persistence. You have a strong sense of self-protection and prefer to stay in your social circle but both men and women need to have a lot of outside support, love and attention. Not great at making big decisions, you tend to be better in advisory roles.

2-3-4:

From the outside you come across as pretty quiet and gentle, as well as being helpful, reliable and diplomatic. Underneath though, there is a sensitive, intense and insightful person with a really expressive and sometimes explosive side which can take others (and you!) by surprise. You really know what you like and don't like, which can make you blind to other factors. Whilst generally conservative in nature, there is a strong impulsiveness about you but you are an insightful observer of people and situations. You can be pretty emotional and will lean on others for strength and support and are likely to develop a pretty thick self-protective wall around you.

2-4-3:

People are likely to describe you as having lots of energy and enthusiasm. Some will say that you are very expressive and spontaneous, sensitive and supportive. Some though might see you as being emotional and at times even aggressive. These two opposites are hard even for you to handle, although you usually get back on an even keel pretty quickly. You are resourceful, self-motivated and assertive but at the same time can be very defensive if asked to take major responsibility for something. There is a very dependent side to your nature, which is particularly evident when an idea or initiative runs out of steam as you tend to be short on stamina and can lose focus.

2-5-2:

Steady, stubborn and serious: you are the type of person who pursues your goals with diligence, persistence, hard work and a good deal of assertiveness. As a result, you will overcome most of the obstacles put in your path. There is real tenderness and a desire to help others but perhaps you can give too much, leaving you unable to focus on your own needs. You don't like to take short cuts but sometimes your meticulous approach means it can take for ever to deal with things. Women will take their role as a mother and a wife very seriously and will want to be in control whilst men need to put aside their pride and be comfortable seeking help and depending on others.

2-6-1:

You are the type of person who has a steady, logical and uncomplicated way of living your life. So much so that for many of you it's a case of "if you can't do it well, there's no point doing it at all". Even though there is great determination in your Natural Expression, there is also a lot of shyness, caution, dependency and insecurity. It may seem paradoxical then that there is great leadership potential where your qualities of thoroughness, prudence, diplomacy and reliability come to the fore. This tends to be a stylish Expression; you may even be a bit of a show-off and there is a strong side of you that is outgoing, excitable and bubbly.

2-7-9:

This is a triple Yin Expression, which sits easily with women, but is more 'complex' for men. For both though, you are going to come across as amusing, entertaining, bubbly, open and easy-going, which will make you popular and fun to be around. At work you are likely to be 'the influencer' rather than 'the leader' and by nature you are intuitive with a real ability to clarify and simplify the issues. You are also good on the detail and have great organisational ability but you can be impulsive and are definitely impressionable. Both men and women will be drawn to Yang Expressions although you might find their 'hardness' difficult to handle in the long term.

2-8-8:

You could describe this Natural Expression as wilful and even though that is too simplistic, it's not that far off. You are serious, bright, ambitious and self-motivated. But at times you are also impulsive and stubborn as well as being dependent and easily influenced. You sometimes can't finish what you started or continue to drive forward when you should really change course. You can get really finicky about details, have a rather short temper and can be very direct with your arguments. Generally though you are a supportive, reliable and kind person but a lot more sensitive and shy than you let on and you can let pride and suspicion get in the way of successful relationships.

2-9-7:

You are a type of person who prefers going out rather than staying in. A varied social life is important to you especially if it's underpinned by style, intellect and creativity. However, at times you can be indiscreet, impulsive, moody and self-centred. You are perceptive and able to see behind people's masks and take a logical and rational view on the situation. As a rule, you are conservative on financial matters but will have bursts of extravagant spending and enjoy showing it off. You make shrewd strategic planners but are not that great at implementing the plans you come up with. You are also a persuasive speaker, especially if there is an audience you want to impress.

Thunder Expressions

Number: 3 **Force**: Yang
Phase: Wood **Family Member**: Eldest Son
Season: Spring **Time of Day**: Dawn

What kind of person you are:
* Explosive * Creative * Impatient * Vibrant * Sensitive * Intense * Determined * Single-Minded * Aggressive * Assertive * Talkative * Passionate * Outgoing * Vibrant * Forthright * Insightful * Rash * Impulsive

Relationships: 3 with 1: Child-Parent (Yang/Yang)
3 with 2: Compatible Opposites (Yang/Yin)
3 with 3: Friendship (Yang/Yang)
3 with 4: Friendship (Yang/Yin)
3 with 5: Conflict Opposites (Yang/Yang)
3 with 6: Conflict Opposites (Yang/Yang)
3 with 7: Passive Control (Yang/Yin)
3 with 8: Conflict Opposites (Yang/Yang)
3 with 9: Parent-Child (Yang/Yin)

Generally Speaking

3 Thunder is the most Yang of all the Expressions and as a result you have huge amounts of drive and natural vibrancy. It leads you to all sorts of places, activities and experiences which you will tend to pursue in short bursts with real zeal and determination but then will relatively quickly lose patience and interest and move onto something else. But if you can maintain your focus, and because you are so goal orientated, you will usually find success, especially when young.

Unsurprisingly, you tend to be assertive leaders with little patience for people who try to block your way or question your direction or motives. You rarely stand down and this assertiveness can develop into aggression and you may use force to get your own way. You need to be the centre of attention, where everything revolves around you and if it doesn't you will quickly go quiet and feel hurt, because actually you are very sensitive.

You are really goal focussed and will quickly (probably too quickly, as you want to run before you can walk) rise to leaderships roles in commerce or public service and use your energy and intelligence as highly effective strategists or planners. In actual fact, you are a natural rebel but can become valued team members as long as you are the first amongst equals. You are likely to be honest and open but are often blunt and unthinking too and will struggle to understand why you are upsetting people around you.

This is a spring Expression and giving life is natural for you. This will range from children to cooking to creative arts to social activities. As a rule, you are not materialistically driven or that interested in keeping things for the sake of it and you will zealously pursue a cause which can be for the greater good for the many or highly focused for your own personal sense of justice. Either way, people will want you on their side, definitely not against you!

Males:

As this is the most masculine of all the Expressions, it suits the male psyche well. But in a way sometimes too well as it doesn't take that much to accentuate the perceived 'negative' connotations of the male gender. Nevertheless, like the 6 Expression (but very different in how it manifests itself), you are a natural born leader although your particular brand of charisma can alienate as much as inspire.

You need to win and be first at everything and will want everyone to know how successful you are usually as a result of your own self-publicity and regardless if anyone is actually interested. But more than anyone else, you can enact change and are a true revolutionary. You are the pioneer and the hot-shot entrepreneur, the breath of fresh air with new ideas and methods which combined with your sharp wit, intelligence and thought provoking style will overcome any obstacle to get things done.

You love adventure and the thrill of the chase and your impulsive behaviour is a real boon in the right circumstances but you will lose your focus and get frustrated if you don't achieve you goals pretty quickly which may then turn your assertiveness into aggressive anger in a flash of light. You're a bit like a puppy, which for short periods of time can be noisy and playful, boisterous even, but then falls into tired exhaustion recharging their batteries ready for the next onslaught!

Typical of all Yang, you like attention and to show off in the way that you dress and look. Like the thunder, that could well be in a shocking or loud manner but you hate being restrained, so prefer clothing that is loose and free.

When it comes to women, you tend to objectify them, often treating them as mere pawns on a chess board. For Yin females, this may not be such a problem as they naturally connect with Yang and need to be led by them; but for Yang females it is likely to be a real problem and conflict and a battle of wills is rarely far away.

Females:

Whilst the 3 Expression suits the man well, for women it is a complex and sometimes difficult one; hardly surprising as it is the most Yang of all the Expressions. The 'mistake' you might make is to try to shield your Natural Expression thinking it is the soft Yin female role you should take on believing this is what society wants you to be. But you are naturally expansive and expressive and trying to hold that in for any length of time will have potentially dire consequences for both your physical and mental health.

Submissive wallflowers you are not! You like and need to be in charge and calling the shots, which career wise can lead you into difficulties unless you are the boss. As leaders you tend to behave in one of two ways: either as the visionary creative spark and energiser or the authoritative single-minded dictator. Either way, you'll always want to be at the centre of things but in the heat of the moment are prone to exaggeration and over-dramatization rather than calm assessment.

You like to dress to impress and have a great eye for design and what looks good, not only to attract the opposite sex but also to elbow out any female competition. Striking, more often than classically beautiful, you draw people towards you using your hypnotic charm to get what you want.

Sadly, you are likely to feel very misunderstood, both generally in society and by those on the outskirts of your social or work circles. But you'll be greatly admired and appreciated by those in your inner circle, where your energy and insight inspires and guides, but you are unlikely to hang around for too long in difficult situations.

You are naturally assertive but if challenged can react aggressively and with real out-of-control anger. This can just as quickly turn inwards especially if you feel ashamed or have taken offense. For Thunder Expressions you need to let go rather than to hold in. The truth is you are highly sensitive, which can be detrimental to your own well-being but that does allow you to pick up nuances in situations and relationships that others may miss. More than anything you need to be calm and grounded and will be naturally drawn to Yin males.

Sex:

Of all the Expressions, you probably have the strongest sex drive of them all and it's likely to be spontaneous, energetic and highly expressive. Also more than the others, you will be open to exploring new and different ways of making love as well as your own sexuality and this is likely to become apparent from an early age. This physical intensity can be overwhelming though and if left unchecked thoughts of sex can dominate your life to detrimental effect.

Love:

Physical, tactile relationships are very important to you but so is your independence, which can lead to you having many love affairs. How you look is really important, which can make the males vain and the females jealous and competitive. Your intensity and high sex drive can make for exciting relationships but equally it can be hard for others to keep up with you both physically and emotionally. Underneath all this activity though, you are a sensitive and loving person wanting to give your all to your relationships.

9-Energy Natural Expressions:

3-1-7:

You are likely to be determined, energetic, industrious and happy to take on lots of commitments but your approach to life is laid-back and easy-going, which ultimately might prevent you fulfilling your ambitions. You come across as straightforward, charming, outgoing and sociable but underneath you are sensitive and somewhat insecure and will only share your true thoughts and emotions with people who've earned your trust. That being said, you are very insightful and can really see and hear people, putting them at ease and making them feel valued. You tend to believe in the 'perfect relationship' and 'true love' and find it hard to compromise which might make it difficult to sustain long-term relationships.

3-2-6:

One way of looking at you is someone who is well-organised, detail minded, honest and direct. The other way is someone who can be overbearing, inflexible, stubborn and self-important. Responsible and hard-working with lots of energy, you are great for coming up with new ideas and novel ways to tackle an issue but you can spend a lot of time faffing around and not getting very far even though you know exactly what needs to be done. You are supportive and helpful in relationships but can get hurt easily if you do not feel loved and appreciated. You like being in the spot-light and will smoothly take on the peace-making role in family disputes.

3-3-5:

This is a powerful triple Yang Expression, amongst the most powerful of them all. This is not such an issue for men but can be for women only because this Expression is naturally commanding and controlling and Learned Convention tells us that these are not feminine characteristics. You have to be involved and at the centre of things but you need the support of others, you can't do it all. You are intelligent, shrewd and very hard working with huge amounts of energy, love and passion. You are stubborn, with your likes and dislikes clearly defined and your warrior-like approach means people will want you on their side. You are deeply sensitive and emotional with an explosive and quick temper. Connecting with Yin Expressions will help as long as you listen to them!

3-4-4:

You are confident, helpful and trusting with a quiet and gentle demeanour. Your natural charm goes a long way in social and work circles. You are hard-working, optimistic and energetic. Underneath though there is a lot of emotion and sensitivity and sometimes you can be a bit over the top and rash in what you say and do. You are likely to be an ideas' person but may struggle to make decisions and then stick with them, although once you do, it's likely to be a good one. In relationships, men can be hard to read and will hide a serious and defensive nature with a breezy manner, whilst women are more outspoken and direct and don't like to be controlled.

3-5-3:

One of the strongest Natural Expressions; this is triple Yang and suits the male body well but not so the female. This is an assertive, stubborn, strong-minded Expression, sometimes aggressive, but always bold, determined and demanding. You have lots of ideas and loads of energy and enthusiasm which may well have given you success at an early age. You are impatient and can 'shoot from the lip' not really thinking through the impact of your words and the hurt you can sometimes cause. You have a bright, keen, insightful mind but can find it difficult to find common ground with others because of your controlling nature. Just below the surface, there really is a very sensitive person.

3-6-2:

From the outside you come across as hardworking, reserved and conservative. On the inside, there is a lot of sensitivity, pride and stubbornness. You're naturally intuitive and insightful and whilst you can focus your high energy levels on getting the job done, you do find it hard to adapt to different situations or engage with people who aren't 'on side'. For men that will manifest as being shy and unapproachable; but women on the other hand are more expressive and can demonstrate leadership potential. You like to help people and are happy to get your hands dirty doing so but you can be a bit of a perfectionist and your directness can be unsettling.

3-7-1:

Internally, there is a lot of strength, energy and a hard-working ethic but externally you can appear shy, quiet, indecisive and cautious. Close friends and family will see another side of you which is funny, engaging, entertaining and playful. You're going to be good fun to be with although that might spill over into being rather overbearing, but your insecurity and vulnerability is never far from the surface making you very sensitive to criticism, which will easily hurt and upset you. Patient and well-organised, you're good at coming up with original ideas and concepts and there is a deeply reflective side to you which typically expresses itself in poetry or other types of creative outlets.

3-8-9:

You are a bright, impulsive person and a bit of a show off at times, both in the way you can behave and the clothes you wear: you enjoy the attention and hate not being noticed. You're an optimistic and spontaneous individual, inspirational at times and with lots of underlying energy and ambition to tackle new projects and get things done. Fundamentally, you're gentle, responsible and secure in your own skin but you can come across as immature and almost childish at times. This is because you tend to have a young outlook on life but if things are not going your way, you're likely to retreat into your cave, roll a rock over the entrance and think about what's happened in silent contemplation.

3-9-8:

Ambitious, showy and self-motivated; you are intelligent, hard-working and full of energy. You can also be moody, haughty and vain. Life is a bit of a roller coaster for you, with high highs and low lows and you can flip-flop one way and then another at the drop of a hat: one moment being the star of the show, the next hiding away in your cave. Your ever changing moods can make you impulsive and impatient but at your core is a very sensitive and intuitive person. Money plays a big part in your life and whilst you don't really come across as greedy, you like to keep hold of it and store it safely away.

Wind Expressions

Number: 4
Phase: Wood
Season: Spring

Force: Yin
Family Member: Eldest Daughter
Time of Day: Dawn

What kind of person you are:
* Gentle * Tender * Liberal * Changeable * Affectionate * Adaptable
* Intimate * Stubborn * Imaginative * Emotional * Open * Confident
* Elusive * Impetuous * Easy-mannered * Harmonious * Scattered * Evasive
* Defensive * Sociable * Moody

Relationships: 4 with 1: Child-Parent (Yin/Yang)
4 with 2: Passive Inertia (Yin/Yin)
4 with 3: Friendship (Yin/Yang)
4 with 4: Friendship (Yin/Yin)
4 with 5: Passive Control (Yin/Yang)
4 with 6: Compatible Opposites (Yin/Yang)
4 with 7: Passive Inertia (Yin/Yin)
4 with 8: Passive Control (Yin/Yang)
4 with 9: Parent-Child (Yin/Yin)

Generally Speaking

Wind is Yin and people of this Expression are generally affectionate, loving and tender but like the wind you can't be tied down and can be changeable. You'll blow hot and cold and have the power of a winter's gale or the gentleness of a summer breeze all in the space of a few minutes! You like and need to take care of others and with your smooth manner and easy communication skills this is natural for you. Impulsive and emotional, you will wear your heart on your sleeve but can quickly become defensive, which some will take as being arrogant or condescending.

Many struggle to see your core being or essence and get frustrated by your apparent indecisiveness. This can make relationships difficult because you do need direction from others (particularly from Yang to provide balance) and without it you can feel lost and stuck in the headlights, even though you do have deep-seated desires and beliefs although these can remain deeply hidden. You like to guide and teach in a soft way, quickly gaining the confidence and trust of those around you and enjoy achieving your success by helping others rather than for your own sake.

You are good at cooling situations down in a calm yet commanding manner and have instinctive diplomatic skills. Conversely, you can use these skills and influence to fan the flames inciting people to take action and fight for a cause. These two opposing actions can bewilder those around you, including yourself. You are particularly effective at playing Devil's Advocate and getting into the nooks and crannies of a person's psyche and raising issues where others may fear to tread.

You can't stand being restrained and whilst great at multi-tasking, you can have bursts of impulsiveness and then spread yourself in too many directions and so lack focus on the main task at hand. You give a lot of yourself to others, can be very emotional and will cry easily.

Males:

Being a Yin force this can be 'complex' for a man. With the wind having no substance of its own and being essentially soft, it can mean others may treat you in an almost feminine manner, which in today's alpha male centred world means you may try to compensate for this by magnifying your male attributes. This would be a mistake, as you just need to be your Natural Expression.

Communicating tends to be a strong suit for you, not just with other people in the words you use and how well you can listen but also in areas such as the arts, journalism, advertising or politics. Indeed, anywhere where a message or an emotion can be conveyed to a person who is free to engage with it.

You can easily be swayed by other people's views and emotional state and can change your mind and opinions just like the direction of the wind. You may see this as being pragmatic, adaptable and non-confrontational but others (especially Yang) can be thrown by this and feel you have little substance or staying power.

When single, you can be great flirts, charming women with your smooth and engaging manner. You hate to be tied down and will think nothing of dating any number of women at the same time. However, when you do settle down, you will be loyal and faithful as long as you are given direction and support and this will nearly always come from a Yang female.

You can be both needy and independent (often liking being the 'odd one out') but more than most, you need to listen to your bodies and your emotions and be true to your Natural Expression. You can too easily be swayed by the crowd or the loudest voice or the latest woman in your life but you need to remain free and easy in the way you think and the way you move.

Females:

The soft and gentle Wind Yin Expression suits the female body well and you are likely to be feminine in a cool and reserved sort of way. Whilst not as cool as the 1 Sea or as expressive as any of the Yang Expressions, expressive you most certainly are!

This softness and your engaging communication style can lead you to the caring professions such as psychology, counselling or therapeutic medicine. You tend to be good at analysis and diagnosis and this can take you to General Practice or senior nursing roles. You make good teachers too but you are particularly suited to music, writing, painting, design and photography, anywhere where you can give freedom to your Expression.

Whilst on the outside you might appear to be joyous, you're actually quite serious, even in a sad sort of way and indeed you can be quite emotional and sensitive getting upset and destabilised by the smallest of things. You can cry easily but then recover quickly and get on with life as if nothing has happened. This can confuse the people around you who can never be quite sure what's really going on for you.

To protect yourself, you often run away into your own private world, detached from the pain and abuses of the day-to-day to become emotionless and distant and then react badly if people try to invade your space, however well-intentioned they may be.

As mothers you often struggle when your children are very young. It's the physical aspect of mothering at that early stage that is usually the problem but as your children grow, you grow into the role too, providing extremely well for their emotional, intellectual and practical needs. It's then that the responsibility of mothering sits comfortably with you as your tolerance, kindness and patience makes for a wonderful life teacher!

Sex:

Because of where it sits in the 5 Phases, Wind Expressions have the physical expressiveness of the full bloom of spring and the emotional capriciousness of the wind itself. Combine that with your trusting and spontaneous nature makes you a very impulsive person when it comes to sexual relationships. You tend to take people at face value and struggle to understand why your partner may not be as sincere as you. More than most, you are likely to hop into bed on a first date (your reasoning being if you both fancy each other, why not?) but really you are searching for something more substantial, where trust and loyalty are key.

Love:

If you could allocate an Expression to a Hollywood RomCom, it would be a 4 Wind as you are the true believers in romantic love. For you, there truly is 'the one' out there and when all the stars are aligned fate will do her duty! Who's to say if that's being naïve? But couple that with your physical expressiveness and emotional openness, you are undoubtedly going to be attractive to others. But you're vulnerable and can allow yourself to be easily let down and get hurt and this is because you can project all sorts of wonderful attributes onto your partners and be attracted and fall in love with a vision rather than the reality. This confusion can be damaging for both of you and so clear pragmatic communications are essential. You will also persevere with relationships, probably for too long, hoping for them to come right or whilst waiting for the real 'one' to turn up.

9-Energy Natural Expressions:

4-1-8:

Strong and silent; sincere and serious; stubborn and self-motivated: that's how the outside world is likely to see you. They'll also see an easy-going, sociable and independent person who generally has a fairly philosophical approach to life. You have the ability to influence others in a quiet, calm sort of way but that can turn to controlling if you feel your opinions are not being accepted. You're an intelligent and pragmatic person but not particularly practical and you tend to learn best by trial and error. You're actually quite emotional with almost fairy tale dreams about love and romance but you tend to be shy and keep your cards close to your chest and are reticent about being the first to expose your true feelings.

4-2-7:

This is a triple Yin Expression, which is a natural fit for females who are comfortable with their independence and clarity of thought; but harder for men who tend to display a feminine and soft behaviour, living on emotion rather than rationality. Both genders are emotional, very sensitive and need lots of attention especially on matters of love where you often take more than you give causing potential difficulties in relationships. You're easy-going, tender and charming but underneath fairly self-centred and sometimes even calculating and you can be quite fussy when it comes to details. You're supportive and helpful and have a natural affinity towards beauty and there is also a reflective and philosophical side to you.

4-3-6:

This is a dignified, direct and detail-focussed Expression. You are straightforward, steady and sometimes stubborn. When stressed, there is a quick and explosive temper lurking but if revealed it will tend to be short-lived and then you will show great determination, hard work and a 'tell-it-how-you-see-it' approach to overcome difficulties and challenges. Emotionally, you are a sensitive person with a definite jealous side to your character and because you tend to have such clear likes and dislikes, others can struggle to get through to you for other alternatives to be considered. You can be pretty intense at times and you crave affection but your pride can sometimes stop you from revealing your true hopes and thoughts.

4-4-5:

To others you're going to appear easy-going, pretty soft and affable. But that hides a stubborn and opinionated side to your character and whilst you have loads of 'get-up-and-go' you need lots of attention and admiration to fuel your motivation and creative ambitions. If you don't get this, you're going to feel hurt and anxious and likely to become erratic and change tact which will confuse you and those around you. You do need to seek the patient advice of your supporters to help you with your decision-making but because you can be pretty self-centred and evasive, you can sometimes be insensitive and ride rough-shod over their feelings and views. There is an obsessive potential to your character which comes to the fore when your self-confidence is dented.

4-5-4:

From the outside, you are self-confident, gentle, trusting and supportive. Inside, there is a powerful core of assertiveness, determination and boldness which only really becomes apparent to friends, family and close work colleagues when the pressure is on. You do have a changeable and sometimes even evasive nature but at heart you are someone with a deep sense of justice and compassion for those less fortunate than yourself. You want to do the right thing and help others and that leads you to the social and caring professions. Your natural empathy and insight coupled with your ability to beat the odds can lead you to a leadership or spokesman type role either formally in a work situation or informally in your local community.

4-6-3:

Enthusiastic, energetic and expressive, you are outgoing and spontaneous and appear pretty easy going. But inside, there are the stirrings of an emotional storm making you at times impatient and self-indulgent. This can make it hard for you to consider others and because you are so straightforward, trusting and proud, you can be taken advantage of. When motivated and interested in something, you have high levels of concentration and become very single-minded and enthusiastic. You are probably too self-critical but conversely hate being criticised by others. You have sound judgement but can be inflexible when circumstances change and you are the person for the big project or deal, not so much in the details.

4-7-2:

For men, this triple Yin Expression can be difficult and you are likely to come across as a bit of worrier and preoccupied with the smallest of details. For women, you are very self-assertive and have a very clear and defined view on where you are going in life, especially if it's family related. For both sexes, you have a tender and gentle nature but you are also self-conscious, emotional and sensitive. This can make you care too much about other peoples' opinions and react badly if you feel you have been misjudged. Being so powerfully Yin, you need the help and direction of Yang Expressions to help you get started on projects but then your steady and natural organisational ability will see you through.

4-8-1:

You are ambitious and hard working with a keen and active mind but you can come across as cautious and reserved, rather insecure and indecisive. However, when you are feeling more secure and comfortable, there is a very sociable and outgoing side to you, although sometimes you will resort to low-level manipulation to get what you want. When feeling insecure, you will worry and often try to assuage your anxiety through self-indulgence such as food, shopping or sex. Your single-mindedness can become obsessive and you have difficulty compromising but you are good with money and have a tender and caring heart when you are feeling confident in a loving relationship.

4-9-9:

Whilst this triple Yin Expression hates to be controlled, the truth is you are very dependent on others (especially Yang) for attention, affection, admiration and a call to action. Your usually expressive actions however may not be what you are really feeling and this can make you appear moody, which actually you probably are. You have high powers of persuasion and influence and can see and get to the point of an issue quickly and then clarify it simply for others. But if your advice is not followed you can get easily hurt and upset for you need to be wanted. You are very tactile, warm and affectionate, sensitive too: but stubborn, fickle and impulsive. You are also intuitive and creative but can easily be blown of course.

Earth Core Expressions

Number: 5
Phase: Earth
Season: Late Summer/Early Autumn
Force: Yang
Family Member: Seventh Child
Time of Day: Afternoon

What kind of person you are:
* Controlling * Bold * Assertive * Strong * Obstinate * Capable * Dogged * Self-centred * Determined * Benevolent * Egotistical * Self-important * Aggressive * Destructive * Practical * Self-Assured * Rigid * Fatalistic * Indomitable

Relationships: 5 with 1: Conflict Opposites (Yang/Yang)
5 with 2: Friendship (Yang/Yin)
5 with 3: Conflict Opposites (Yang/Yang)
5 with 4: Passive Control (Yang/Yin)
5 with 5: Friendship (Yang/Yang)
5 with 6: Parent-Child (Yang/Yang)
5 with 7: Parent-Child (Yang/Yin)
5 with 8: Friendship (Yang/Yang)
5 with 9: Child-Parent (Yang/Yin)

Generally Speaking

The 5 Earth Core Expression is different from the others. As discussed in Chapter 3 of this part of the book, it is not represented by a family member (and so is often referred to as the Seventh Child) and is a result of a vortex of Yin and Yang and is said to be at the centre of the Earth. Consequently, it is considered the most powerful Expression of them all. (Remember, that is not a good or bad thing, or means it's better or worse than any other Expression: it's just what it is).

The 5 needs to be at the centre of things and because you have the talent and the determination to match, you're going to be admired and respected by those around you. It makes for strong men and strong women. Whilst you are the most self-sufficient of the Expressions, you do need the right people around you and you must listen to them; but while you can and will adapt, it will usually only be on your terms and in truth actual change is rare. You constantly like to try new things and give the impression you are changing - and will go on and on telling everyone about it - but real change? Of course it's possible, but not that likely.

Easily bored and more practical than intellectual, you believe you are right virtually all of the time, and even when you're proved wrong, you still believe you are right! You need to be in control of everything and everyone around you and see yourself as an utter failure if you're not. This boldness and air of invulnerability can leave people dumbfounded requiring their patience and understanding to figure out what's really going on.

Usually, you have a wide social circle and network well in business and in the corridors of power. You tend to have a fatalistic approach to life and seek a 'return' on your 'investment', be it socially, romantically, politically or career-wise but your tendency to over analyse can see you going round and round in circles. You tend to be very honest – brutally so at times – and whilst you can talk a hind leg off a donkey, it's action, not smooth platitudes that drives you forward.

Males:

If you had to choose one word to sum up the 5 Expression for a man, it's power! You want to control people, and woe betide anyone if they try to control you as they're sure to fail. You don't really need anyone either, as this is a self-sufficient and egocentric Expression, which means you'll happily plough your own furrow and 'use' the people you connect with (which you do easily, both socially and professionally) to gain power over them. To you, asking for help will be seen as a failure which both limits your progress and isolates you.

You are going to be a proud, even pretentious person who see things in a pretty black and white way and can be quite dismissive of other Expressions and what they offer and stand for. Undeniably reliable and practical, you may appear to move or change your position but actually it's only within your own narrow band and in a rather mechanical way as well. You take more than you give and are accumulators (money, knowledge, experiences from the past) and don't like to let go.

This is a very physical Expression, which can be seen in your keen sense of humour (visual, slapstick sort of style) and in the bedroom, where your power is shown through the body rather than a spiritual connection. Whilst this can generally have a pretty negative effect on women, especially strong Yang females, Yin females are drawn to your power and ability to provide and to be looked after, although this can turn easily and quickly into being controlled.

You are very aware of your image and like to look good in a powerful, look-at-me sort of way and whilst you know an awful lot (and like telling everyone you know an awful lot), deep analytical thinking is not really your forte. You like to be noticed in whatever career you choose, which often means your own business or in a high profile executive role.

Females:

Like the male 5s, women of this Expression are all about control and power and dominance over both females and males (particularly Yin males). 5 Earth Core is a Yang Expression and therefore 'complex' for a woman but like the 2 Earth Yin Expression, it is also maternal but a lot less Yin in nature.

You're likely to be very confident and believe totally in your own self-sufficiency and ability to power through whatever the situation. This egocentric approach might work for you in certain circumstances but because you so often refuse to ask for help or advice, you usually find yourself isolated and alone. This is to your detriment, and also to those around you, because it means your natural leadership skills are not being used for the benefit of all. Your regal demeanour demands respect and lends you a natural authority, which can be found from the boardroom to the home.

It's true you can be manipulative and self-serving and if people don't bend to your will, you will cut them off without a second thought. But you can also be very considerate and generous both with your time and possessions, although that might come at a price further down the road as you may be looking for something in return.

You will decide who you want as a partner and will use your body, clothes and physical power to attract the man you want and be at the centre of their attention. It's likely you'll have many male admirers but you'll want to control and use them to get what you want, which may be money, power or possessions.

You are wonderful providers to your children (especially your favourites) and if you can get the attention of being 'the mum behind the star' so much the better! You are definitely not the 'behind-the-scenes' mother a 2

Earth Expression is likely to be. You are ferociously determined to get what you want for yourself, your children and your man, but actually mostly for yourself.

Sex:

Sex is really important to 5 Earth Core Expressions and you need to have a partner who can match your physicality and passion - just as long as it is you who is in control and at the centre of things. You can be demanding and domineering in bed which can lead to all sorts of unusual and audacious positions, both literally and figuratively! But it can also make you sexually over-dependant on your lover and whilst you really do want to please your partner, if you continually refuse to listen to them or not be patient and accommodating to their needs, it can lead to a damaging and unhappy situation and a likely break down of the relationship.

Love:

Finding a partner is not usually that difficult for a 5 Expression as you exude a strong physical attractiveness but you also like and need a lot of variety which can lead to infidelity. But these potential acts of unfaithfulness usually fall into the 'No Big Deal' category, as you remain deeply committed to your partner and it is more to do with proving to yourself that you are still attractive rather than dissatisfaction with your relationship. It can make for some interesting love triangles though! Partners of 5 Expressions need to be tolerant and understanding to your extremes for in reality you are a very caring, loving and honest person.

9-Energy Natural Expressions:

5-1-9:

There is a kind of flamboyant, impulsive air about you and you don't mind showing off how clever and creative you are or making a statement by the way you dress. You're better at leading than following and you have high principles but you can struggle to get across what you actually stand for and expect from your followers. There are times when you can be cautious and withdrawn but mostly you're at the centre of things where your energy, focus and ambition are put to best use. You're not great at showing your emotions and can be pretty defensive on matters of the heart. You're also pretty hopeless at reading signals, especially from your partner or colleagues if the issue is personal rather than work related.

5-2-8:

You are the sort of person who is really good at helping and supporting others, especially if they are vulnerable or close to you in the family or at work. But you do really want to control them and be at the centre of their lives until the issue is resolved as you see it. Yes, you're pretty inflexible and stubborn, but you're determined and ambitious, idealistic too. How you look and come across is important to you but that can become a bit flashy and fussy. Trying to control you is really hard, so it's surprising perhaps that you are actually pretty dependent on others both for emotional support and confirmation that you're doing the right thing. Recognition is usually more important than financial reward.

5-3-7:

Socially, you're going to come across as easy-going, fun, straightforward and engaging. You like and need to be at the centre of things wherever that may take you. You are strong willed, assertive, hardworking and controlling. At times, you can be quite explosive especially under intense pressure but you have a lot of energy and ambition to get the things you want, although some may take that as you being greedy and materialistic. You're actually more interested in the achievement than the spoils but if things are not going your way in love or in work, you will look to move quickly on. You like to keep your personal and public lives separate and are pretty black & white about your likes and dislikes.

5-4-6:

Dignified, magnanimous, strong-willed and well-organised, you are really good at controlling things and managing people and will use your logical and straightforward approach to good effect. Others will see you as stubborn and inflexible but always honest and sincere. Underneath your front though there is an impulsive and emotional side that can see you being indecisive and seeking the support and love of those close to you. This will often bewilder them as you like to appear so strong and in control from the outside. In times of trouble, you really come to the fore and your energy and resolute personality will see you overcome most of the obstacles put in your path.

5-5-5:

Not a lot of grey in this powerful triple Yang Expression. All 5 Expressions need to control but this one does it in spades! You are going to have huge amounts of drive, energy, self-motivation and resolve. You don't spend too much time considering those you seek to control and are likely to be demanding and assertive towards them. However, people will tend to gravitate towards you for both support and inspiration and you can be generous, magnanimous and caring as long as they don't cross you! You are direct, bold and intense and you're probably going to be involved and at the centre of everything! But it can be draining to be so strong and very deep inside there is actually nervousness and insecurity that can cause emotional upheaval.

5-6-4:

Your public persona is usually gentle, unassuming, easy-going and smooth talking. But underneath there is a strong will to plough your own furrow and once hooked on something or someone your focus, strong will and high energy is likely to see your ambition come to a successful conclusion especially if there is a materialistic benefit. Generally, you are helpful and dependable with a wide circle of friends and associates but you expect there to be mutual benefits. Controlling by nature, stubborn and rather inflexible, you can be very self-critical needing everything to be just so. There is a significant emotional side to you but you're a survivor and if things are not going your way or you lose interest, you will pragmatically move on.

5-7-3:

Even though the 5 controlling element is never that far away, you are really quite a sensitive person blessed with a reflective perception about what's going on with people and how events might affect their life. You can be hasty, impatient and stubborn and if things are not going your way, you are likely to be inappropriately forceful in trying to assert your will and opinions, which will likely cause difficulties in personal and work relationships. But if you do feel in control, you have an inner security that allows you to be great company: witty, expressive, spontaneous and charming. You are usually very energetic and a really good organiser with a good eye for detail but you can be quite materialistic too.

5-8-2:

You're going to come across as steady, reliable, serious and fairly reserved. Yes, the 5 controlling, ambitious, materialistic and demanding aspects are there too but there is quite a lot of front here because you are a lot more dependent on others than you care to let on. You're likely to play a central part in family and community life where they will find you energetic, friendly and helpful. You have a very tenacious and persistent nature (some will say stubborn), which can really help when getting to the heart of matters but can also make you uncommunicative and close-minded if having to consult with others. When you're feeling secure though, there is a real, almost naïve, charm about you.

5-9-1:

There is a lot of drive and energy here to get what you want out of life, especially if it involves fame and the money and possessions that go with it. The conflict is that you are a lot more shy and indecisive than you want to admit and this struggle between the dreams and the reality can cause difficulties. Whilst you can be rather impulsive, you are persistent and strong-willed with loads of ambition but you do need to be at centre of things to deflect that nagging sense of insecurity you sometimes have. You enjoy your social life where you can display your affectionate and playful nature and you can be very inspiring, creating and effectively delivering presentations and speeches.

Sky Expressions

Number: 6
Phase: Metal
Season: Late Autumn
Force: Yang
Family Member: Father
Time of Day: Evening

What kind of person you are:
* Organised * Principled * Magnanimous *Loyal * Dignified * Rational * Proud * Stylish * Cautious * Perfectionist * Unflustered * Resolute * Reasoned * Rigid * Noble * Uncompromising * Directing * Inflexible * Courteous * Gallant * Coherent

Relationships: 6 with 1: Parent-Child (Yang/Yang)
6 with 2: Child-Parent (Yang/Yin)
6 with 3: Conflict Opposites (Yang/Yang)
6 with 4: Compatible Opposites (Yang/Yin)
6 with 5: Child-Parent (Yang/Yang)
6 with 6: Friendship (Yang/Yang)
6 with 7: Friendship (Yang/Yin)
6 with 8: Child-Parent (Yang/Yang)
6 with 9: Passive Control (Yang/Yin)

Generally Speaking

There is nothing bigger than the sky and this Yang Expression is powerful, noble and complete. Highly organised with an efficient and clear thinking mind, you are able to overcome difficult and challenging times in a steadfast and calm thinking manner. Although this calm approach can sometimes, and quite quickly, turn to over cautiousness and defensiveness resulting in lost opportunities.

It would seem with this type of Expression that you would take to social situations like a duck to water but actually the opposite is usually true. Yes, you can put on a good show and appear charismatic and engaging but really it's hiding a rather calculating side to your character. This is because you can be so direct and intense, which occasionally offends those around you as you seem not to care about their needs or feelings. You don't mean it; it's just the way you can sometimes come across.

You like to have things your own way, which is fine up to a point but because you can struggle to compromise and show flexibility, you can find yourself isolated and alone. You also tend to keep your cards close to your chest and so whilst never being dishonest, there is a good chance you won't actually tell people what you're really feeling. Also, whilst things may all look cool and poised on the outside, it can mask a brewing storm which can suddenly erupt taking people by surprise and even frightening you.

You're the kind of Chairman of the Board, High Court Judge or Lord of the Manor type character, whose ability to see and understand the big picture with a rational and calm approach allows you to summarise, advise and dispense judgement in a powerful, structured and dignified way. Whilst you can be generous, you do have a tendency to be a little bit too money orientated and your great sense of pride can be both an advantage and a disadvantage.

Males:

This Expression suits the male body well because it is Yang and truly masculine. It is also represented as the Father at the family table, so this is an Expression that is powerful yes, but in a paternal, dignified and understated sort of way. You are the King, comfortable on your throne, not needing to prove anything to anyone. You can be attentive, generous and charismatic charmers when you choose to be but others beware: you are assertive, controlling and usually looking to gain something out of the situation or from the people around you. It makes for a side to your character that is hard, cold and mechanical. You are a strong, challenging personality, believing you are always right and can quite easily display the less savoury male attitudes towards women, sex, possessions and money.

You love to be socially well connected and to show off how successful and powerful you are in what you wear, the woman on your arm and the car that you drive. (All of these will be stylish and in good taste, never flashy or loud).

You tend to be very physical and body orientated. You will typically like sports and be very good at them, especially if it means you can show off your body and be the captain of the team. In a fight for a woman or a business deal, you are a tough competitor and will take risks especially if the spoils are high.

Yang is brittle though and never more so than with a male 6 Expression. Yes you are a leader but because you rarely ask for help, or trust the people around you, your ego mind can take over making you isolated and lonely. In these circumstances, rather than seeking balance in Yin, you will instead push ever further with the power games which eventually will cause you much unhappiness and illness.

Females:

For the female, this is one of the most 'complex' Expressions. Like your male counterparts, you are natural leaders and carry yourself with an easy authority and dignified manner. Proud, demanding, even arrogant, you are brave, logical and will argue anyone to a standstill that black is white and white is black to demonstrate you are right, however obvious to everyone else that you are not. For you, it is all about power and control and getting your own way and if that means bending or breaking a few rules on the way, so be it.

One of your biggest issues is how you deal with the men in your life and your relationship with them. Not in a physical beauty sense because as a rule you are strong, sexy, elegant and striking, but because in one way or another, the man will always get it wrong! He will either get in the way of your career and leadership ambitions or he will come onto you in an inappropriate romantic sense. Similar to the 3 female, it is you that must do the approaching and take the lead and this is especially true dealing with Yin males, who must put their male ego mind away and let you do the 'work'.

Being a Sky Expression, it is not surprising that you are very spatially aware and like the male 6 will be drawn to architecture, planning and design as well as art and sculpturing. Medicine suits you well too, especially as a leading surgeon and because you are so body conscious and expressive, any type of dancing will be natural for you, especially if you are the star of the show!

You are also natural mothers but perhaps in a more fatherly sense because it will be you who will dispense the discipline and ensure your children are well behaved, even if you are not around a lot of the time due to work or other commitments. But you are utterly devoted to your children and will look after them with genuine warmth, kindness and patience.

Sex:

There is a very strong sex drive associated with 6 Expressions and as a rule it is straightforward, conventional and somewhat reserved. You tend to have a rather defined view of what is appropriate or not i.e. where, when and how. Whilst on the outside, you may seem quietly confident and self-assured, you can put too much importance on 'performance' and if that is questioned (either by your partner or by self-criticism), it can be devastating. For both genders, you are going to be sexually very powerful and usually take the dominant position, which Learned Convention says is OK for a man and not so OK for a woman. It is of course, OK for both.

Love:

Similar to your sex lives, 6 Expressions seek well defined love relationships and you are likely to be direct about what you want and don't want and what is morally right and wrong. You are a devoted and loving partner and an effective and reliable provider of both emotional and practical needs. In difficulties however, men can try to dominate their partners either overtly by aggressive behaviour or passively by appearing weak and needy. You hate to be thought of as failures, so may well end up doing all sorts of jobs and tasks being at the beck and call of your partner. Women on the other hand can feel over obliged to take on more and more responsibilities which if allowed to build-up will eventually overcome you.

9-Energy Natural Expressions:

6-1-1:

There are two very definite sides to this Expression: on the one hand you will blow people away with your extrovert, fun, passionate and witty way of being; and on the other there is the withdrawn, insecure, indecisive and cautious person. Both are real but the former you like to show; the latter you only reveal to those close to you, and as a triple Yang Expression, you are probably going to be more comfortable confiding with Yin Expressions. You are strong-willed, tenacious, magnanimous and assertive and you can

Sex, Love and Who Puts the Rubbish Out?

be really inspiring and influential with a warrior type leadership potential. You are also a bit of a diplomat, particularly effective at tactful negotiations within your family and close circle of friends.

6-2-9:

There's an impulsive and flamboyant side to your character and when that is coupled with your strong sense of pride and firm work ethic, you often find yourself gravitating towards leadership roles. You're not a great follower and are often very direct, but you can get overconfident and sometimes seem rather conceited and unapproachable. That is a shame, because your natural urge is to help and support people and you are really good at smoothing troubled waters with an easy but commanding sense of tact and diplomacy. Well organised, good at planning and detail conscious (perhaps too detail conscious), you are usually a pretty calm person and actually quite cautious in your dealings with people and situations.

6-3-8:

If you are a man, this triple Yang Expression sits pretty comfortably with you and your sensitivity is often expressed by caring about others. For women though, this air of independence, ambition, drive and using other people to get what you want is, by the Learned Convention of today, seen as rather unfeminine but as we know Learned Convention is tosh! Either way, both males and females are hard-working, direct, self-motivated and opinionated. You are also usually very expressive and potentially explosive, although the storm tends to clear pretty quickly. You have high moral principles which you are reluctant to compromise on and whilst you are by nature forward looking and insightful, you can sometimes be surprisingly cautious missing opportunities as a result.

6-4-7:

You are a personality that changes easily (perhaps too easily) from being affable, charming, easy-going and confident to one that is impulsive, strong, stubborn and emotional. This is hard enough for you to get your head around let alone trying to explain your thoughts to others and this often makes it hard for you to plan and take important decisions. You have high ideals, take pride in what you do and how you come across and like to have that recognised by those around you. You have a tender heart and a trusting nature, which is typically reciprocated, but you are forthright in your dealings with people and like all the 6s have a strong capacity for leadership and inspiring those around you.

6-5-6:

This is a strong and independent triple Yang Expression and so you are likely to be self-assured, strong-willed and ambitious with an easy confidence to comfortably take on leadership roles. You are going to be reliable, direct, well-organised and rational with high moral principles. The flipside to that is being stubborn, pig-headed, overbearing and egotistical. You like positions of high responsibility and need to be in control and if you're not your sense of pride and importance can really take a hit. You can easily become over-confident (but not be aware of it) and simply dismiss the views and opinions of those around you to your own detriment. There is however, a sort of stylish elegance about you, understated but powerful.

6-6-5:

A powerful triple Yang Expression and one that would be termed 'simple' for a man and 'complex' for a woman and that's because this Expression is about leading rather than following, as your pride and natural assertiveness prevents you comfortably taking orders or accepting alternative ideas. On the outside, you are bold and determined, single-minded and inflexible, but internally a lot more sensitive and cautious than you want to let on. You are self-critical, highly focused, logical, prudent and well-organised and take the view that if the job's not worth doing well, it's not worth doing at all. You want to be at the centre of things and in control of it all and that can make you appear domineering and obsessive.

6-7-4:

As with all 6's, you have the potential to lead but your Yin numbers (7,4) tempers the controlling and domineering aspects, so you're likely to come across as gentle, easy-going, magnanimous and considerate. Your close friends and associates will find a witty and fun person to be with but

Sex, Love and Who Puts the Rubbish Out?

outsiders may see a different side which can be forceful, brash and thoughtless. This is because whilst you can be reflective, you are typically very sensitive and can overreact inappropriately if you feel slighted. You tend to expend a lot of energy and focus when you have settled on a particular plan of action and you can be very effective at politics. There is an easy and comfortable style about you, although at times you can be very self-conscious.

6-8-3:

There is a sort of stylish dignity about this triple Yang Expression and couple that with an outward show of enthusiastic energy and expressive emotions means you are likely to be very popular and socially in demand. You tend to be either 'on' or 'off' with not a lot in between; and when you're 'off' you will prefer to hide away and be very private, rather shy and uncommunicative. You believe in high morals and standards and are very considerate and generous to those close to you but likely to ignore those who aren't. You are direct, have a lot of pride and ambition, and have the ingredients to make an inspiring leader. You can be rash and impatient though and that can have a detrimental effect on achieving your goals.

6-9-2:

There is an air of self-confidence, boldness and even daring-do about you and combine that with your persistence and diligence means you are likely to achieve your goals and unlikely to accept second-best. Your social, engaging and easy-going manner can hide real ambition and a strong will, which along with a good dose of impulsiveness will tend to be exposed when you're under stress. You can be vain and moody and rather self-centred and at times inconsiderate to those around you with the result that the undoubted potential you have for inspiring leadership can be badly dented. This can also affect your decision-making which can become hesitant, inconsistent and sometimes impractical.

Lake Expressions

Number: 7 **Force:** Yin
Phase: Metal **Family Member:** Youngest Daughter
Season: Late Autumn **Time of Day:** Evening

What kind of person you are:
* Polished * Inventive * Cool * Enigmatic * Nervy * Passionate * Sensitive * Expressive * Joyous * Easy-going * Reflective * Calculating * Spiritual * Adaptable * Talkative * Social * Elegant * Refined * Quick-witted *Analytical

Relationships: 7 with 1: Parent-Child (Yin/Yang)
7 with 2: Child-Parent (Yin/Yin)
7 with 3: Passive Control (Yin/Yang)
7 with 4: Passive Inertia (Yin/Yin)
7 with 5: Child-Parent (Yin/Yang)
7 with 6: Friendship (Yin/Yang)
7 with 7: Friendship (Yin/Yin)
7 with 8: Child-Parent (Yin/Yang)
7 with 9: Passive Inertia (Yin/Yin)

Generally Speaking

As befits a Lake Expression, you can look bright and sparkly on the surface but who knows what lurks underneath? It's usually deeply held passions and emotions, which most will miss because they will be dazzled by your playful and social exterior and unless you choose otherwise, that's exactly the way Lake Expressions want it to be.

You have a sharp mind and a quick wit and because you are natural entertainers can speak well in most situations, so long as you can control your nervousness which is never far from the surface. Because you are good at hiding your true feelings, you can come across as insincere and self-serving and not entirely straightforward. That being said, you are really good at empathising and instinctively sensing the real issues and are wonderful friends in difficult times offering clear and grounded advice and a shoulder to cry on.

Being a Yin Expression, you are both flexible and easy-going and adaptable to change but need the direction and guidance of others (especially Yang) to help you set firm foundations. This is especially true in your early years because if you were over-indulged as a child and allowed to set your own agenda, you may well be spoiled, stuck-up and rather conceited.

You are natural optimists but couple that with a distinct lack of persistence can lead to many projects and ambitions being left unfinished or unfulfilled. You are attracted to elegant refinement which gives you a natural affinity with interior design and classic style. More than any of the other Expressions, you are open to a deep spiritual connection and a stillness of the mind.

Males:

Lake is the most Yin of the Expressions and as it is also associated with the youngest daughter, it makes this a very 'complex' Expression for a man. In male company, you will often attempt to overcome the depth of your Yin by being over masculine, loud and competitive especially when it comes to the quick-witted rejoinder which is often cutting and unerringly to the point. In female company on the other hand, you are charming, warm, cheeky and playful – a real ladies man in a metrosexual sort of way.

On the surface, you can be cool, calculating and critical with a self-righteous and distrustful air about you. You have your own code of morality and it gives you a sense of control and power which in a leadership role is often misplaced as you are a lot more effective as a No 2 or taking on a specialist role such as in law or education.

You ooze refinement and style but in an understated yet classy sort of way and enjoy being with cool people in cool places surrounded by cool possessions. This can lead to careers in fashion, design and architecture.

The complexity of your Yin male Expression means you can effortlessly follow a deeply meditative path to find calm, stillness and peace, which could literally save you as underneath the bright shining extrovert can lie depression, bewilderment and suffering.

Females:

Lake suits the female body well and this is something you instinctively feel in a physical, sexual and spiritual sense for you can attain a deep clarity and stillness if you find freedom from your inner conflict and live by your Natural Expression. But if that doesn't happen, you can become very internally controlled and vulnerable to falling into a state of obsessive compulsion. Your Natural Expression is really that of your inner self; resilient, cool and unemotional up to a point but not that far from the surface, susceptible to anguish and distress.

You can be childlike, naïve even and innocent to the realities of the world which means you can easily be taken advantage of and whilst you can appear bright, joyous and sexually flirtatious, it is often hiding nervousness and insecurity. You are probably a stickler for following rules and regulations and you don't like being told what to do. You can show a strong stubborn and rebellious streak when you want to, which can get you into difficult places if you behave rashly.

You like to feel morally correct and will go to any lengths and pay any price if you believe in the cause you are standing for. But outsiders are unlikely to see much of that pain or emotional cost as it will likely be hidden behind a smiling face and a shrug of the shoulders. Sometimes you can be seen as being manipulative but if that is the case it's really just their difficulty with your direct style of communication. Because this is a feminine Yin Expression, Yang men will be drawn to you and you tend to get on well with Yang females because there are fewer issues when it comes to leadership in the relationship.

You like structure, order and form with everything neatly packaged and in the right place. Your tastes are refined, simple and straightforward: wacky and off-the-wall is not really your style, but as you age, you might come across as being a bit too prim and proper!

You make great mothers and really enjoy playing with your children (sometimes being hard to tell you apart!). Being needed, helping and giving guidance and direction are really important to you.

Sex:

Sensuous, sensitive and subtle, 7 Expressions need love-making to be perfect, delicate and exquisite. You are very responsive to your partner's needs and desires and want nothing more than to give them pleasure. Because 7 is so Yin, Yang Expressions are ideal partners but if a relationship becomes stagnant, you are likely to move on quickly showing little patience in trying to work things through. These same Yang Expressions however may not be as focused on your pleasure as you are on theirs, which might lead to abuse from them and a passive aggressive behaviour from you.

Love:

Because from the outside you appear flirtatious, joyous and charming, you are likely to be very attractive to a potential partner. Your more reflective and spiritual qualities will remain hidden until you are at ease and comfortable that the relationship is just how you want it. And that is often a problem, because your partner may not have the same vision as you do, and you can struggle to adapt or lower your standards. You will want your partner to match your joyous nature and look good and stylish, and whilst you can find it hard to say 'no', your strong independent streak means you can find it difficult to make a long-term commitment.

9-Energy Natural Expressions:

7-1-2:

You tend to be very comfortable in social situations and have the makings of the perfect host. That's because you have an easy-going, extrovert, witty and charming personality with that knack of making people feel at ease and important. But unless they are close to you, it's unlikely they will see your sensitive side which can sometimes make you seem cautious, withdrawn and uncommunicative. They might also miss your philosophical and reflective insights and observations, but all are likely to feel the benefits of your helpful and supportive attitude. You tend to live your life and base a lot of your decisions on intuition and a gut instinct but you are actually quite conservative and at times obstinate.

7-2-1:

You are likely to come across as a person who is rather quiet and quite shy. It may seem at odds then that actually you are often craving attention but if your sensitivity gets the better of you, it can make you needy and insecure. What's hiding underneath is a thoughtful and reflective individual who can make sound judgements with a steady, resourceful and pragmatic approach. Some might see that as being indecisive but actually you are just being cautious and coolly calculating. You are good in social situations and can make people feel at ease using your charm, sense of humour and natural enthusiasm for life. You like to get to know how people are really feeling and thinking deep down and you would like that to be reciprocated.

7-3-9:

You are hardworking, determined and resourceful but you can also add flashes of brilliance, not only for new ideas and ways of doing things, but also by shedding light on existing issues and situations. You can be quite inspirational and because you are also bright and articulate, you make a persuasive communicator and are likely to attract people keen to be a part of whatever project you happen to be involved in. You don't like to hide your feelings and despite having an open and flexible attitude, you have a strong sense of right and wrong and likes and dislikes. You are good at reading people because you are very sensitive but can get frustrated because you long for affection and attention from those close to you.

7-4-8:

You combine the qualities of charm, resourcefulness and self-confidence with tenacity, prudence and a steady caution. You tend to be popular in your social circle but your public affability can mask a stubborn and inflexible side unwilling to play along to someone else's tune. You usually take your time to settle on a final course of action, often changing your mind frequently before you get there, but once done, it's done and you don't give up easily. You can be pretty emotional and sensitive and that can play a large part in your life and the decisions you make. Your default is to trust people and you expect them to trust you in return, and to those close to you, you are caring and considerate.

7-5-7:

It can look like there are three sides to this Expression: on one there is a demanding, assertive and strong willed individual; on another there is a fun-loving, charming and sociable person; and on the third side someone who can be hypersensitive, defensive and easily influenced. Whatever is on show at the time, you are someone who doesn't like to fit in with convention, can keep a cool head when the pressure is on and who usually achieves more doing your own thing rather than being part of a team. There is an air of idealistic innocence about you, which can leave you exposed to being taken for a ride but you have great foresight and the easy ability to put people at ease and be considerate to their views.

7-6-6:

There is a dignified style and easy charm about you. You take pride in how you carry yourself and back your own intuition and instincts. You have a confident, logical and straightforward approach to life but your sensitivity and emotions play a large part too. That can affect your leadership potential but your energy, focus and enthusiasm usually sees you achieving your goals and persuading others to follow you. You're not very flexible though – actually you are pretty stubborn – and can struggle to adapt to changing circumstances. On the surface, you usually come across as sincere, serious and direct but you have real passion and ambition to achieve and realise your high ideals.

7-7-5:

You are likely to be the kind of person that has loads of energy, displays enormous self-confidence and works incredibly hard. You are entertaining, funny and sharp, with a lot of natural charm. You can sometimes be a little too detail-conscious for your own good and agonise that you've made the right decisions but you're a great organiser and finisher. You may come across as easy-going and flexible but you need to be in control and to receive lots of praise and attention for your achievements. You have a lot of 'front', but behind it lies much sensitivity, nervousness, self-doubt and insecurity; and criticism of any kind can really dent your confidence. You can both talk and listen well and are perceptive and spiritually inclined.

7-8-4:

On the face of it, you are sociable, charming and good fun to be with. You have a strong independent streak but can be rather ego-centric and defensive. You have a sharp mind - and sometimes a sharp tongue - but you are a good communicator, listen well and can be pretty perceptive. Your flexibility and strong self-motivation allows you to handle most of what life throws up but you can be quite calculating, weighing up the options for your best advantage. There is a deep pool of sensitivity about you and you can be shy and nervous in situations where you feel uncomfortable preferring to retreat to your cave for reflection. Whilst you can be very obstinate, you're really a trusting, gentle person and want to help others.

7-9-3:

You're the sort of person who likes to stand out from the crowd. You're probably a self-confident extrovert with an engaging and cheerful demeanour who wants to be the centre of attention. You can talk for your country but be very persuasive and inspiring at the same time. But your 'front' hides a sensitive and sometimes insecure person, liable to mood swings which at times can be explosive and even aggressive. You hate to be criticised and are vulnerable to flattery. Whilst you are industrious and energetic, you can be pushy and even inconsiderate of others with a degree of impatience that can prevent the completion of projects. You like to break new ground and to receive praise for your achievements.

Mountain Expressions

Number: 8
Phase: Earth
Season: Late Summer/Early Autumn

Force: Yang
Family Member: Youngest Son
Time of Day: Afternoon

What kind of person you are:
* Persistent * Opinionated * Tenacious * Obstinate * Searching
* Single-minded * Revolutionary * Energetic * Focused * Headstrong
* Acquisitive * Bold * Self-motivated * Accumulating * Self-indulgent
* Ambitious

Relationships: 8 with 1: Conflict Opposites (Yang/Yang)
8 with 2: Friendship (Yang/Yin)
8 with 3: Conflict Opposites (Yang/Yang)
8 with 4: Passive Control (Yang/Yin)
8 with 5: Friendship (Yang/Yang)
8 with 6: Parent-Child (Yang/Yang)
8 with 7: Parent-Child (Yang/Yin)
8 with 8: Friendship (Yang/Yang)
8 with 9: Child-Parent (Yang/Yin)

Generally Speaking

The Mountain Expression is Yang and like the mountain you are imposing, impenetrable and immovable. But inside this hard exterior there is actually much softness and gentleness. You tend to find there are two powerful sides to your character: tender and caring; and obstinate and covetous. The first side can make you very popular, well-liked and easy to relate to. The second side can see unscrupulous behaviour where you pursue your own self-interests and will ride rough-shod over other people's feelings. This changing of your mind can make you appear insincere and sometimes lead you to make childish decisions.

Accumulation is an integral part of this Expression. It can manifest in a number of ways: money and possessions; influence and position; emotions and memories. You can harbour many positive and romantic feelings from past relationships but also slights and perceived injustices. Either way, you nearly always manage to get one over the other person and have the last word.

You like to take charge and be in control, are strong and determined and can weather any storm. Brave and loyal, you want to be seen at the centre of social activities, hate the idea of not being liked (unless you're the one doing the disliking) or appearing soft or needy. But if matters take a turn not to your liking, you are not averse to a state of splendid and noble isolation.

Fundamentally, you are conservative and traditional in nature, analytical and very much into your own ideas and individuality. You want to be seen and respected by others but for the most part you need the help and encouragement of someone stronger or more influential than you to get what you really want, but will often let hubris get in the way of asking or even accepting their help.

Males:

As the Mountain Expression is Yang, this connects well with the male body and is stereotypically masculine. This Expression is all about strength, force and physical prowess. Your physical appearance is really important to you, not just in the power and fitness of your body but also in how that power is conveyed. You achieve this by your general demeanour and the clothes you wear such as power suits or military uniform.

Not particularly open to a spiritual way of life, you tend to be practical, down-to-earth types. You are usually charming and attractive in a rough-and-ready sort of way who enjoys and loves the social side of life, where you might find yourself being the captain of the village sports team or chairman of local committees.

You are the type of person who will slowly and methodically reach the top of your own personal metaphorical mountain. On the way up, you'll gain much expertise, knowledge and experience and you're not going to be impressed by people who take short cuts or fluke it to the top.

You can shoot from the lip and come across as insensitive and even chauvinistic and whilst you tend to be rather ego-centric, you are honest, loyal, have good intentions and a kind heart. Regardless of your age, you are really just a big kid, who loves playing with your toys and wants everyone to play along with you.

Females:

When the singer Cat Stevens wrote about looking for a hard-headed woman, he probably had an 8 female in mind! This is a Yang Expression and so whilst not the ideal fit for the female body, there is actually a very soft centre, similar to the male 8, but more so. You can be kind, loving and generous but you can also be very stubborn, stamping your foot if you don't get your way, or even getting aggressive becoming very emotional and physical at the same time.

You love socialising and being the centre of attention. You are fun to be with; friendly, amusing and engaging. You like to be flattered and will use your bodies and how you dress to gain attention and impress an audience or an individual to get what you want. You are usually very ambitious and practical and will comfortably take up a leadership role at work or in a relationship. You can be abrupt and ego-centric and if you feel wronged you will never forget it, for you are a great accumulator of things such as emotions and memories as well as money and possessions. But you can be very loving and passionate towards your partner and kind and generous to those around you, just as long as your needs are met first.

You're pretty conservative by nature and have fixed views and opinions and once you believe in something that's it! Change can happen but often you think you've changed in some significant way and want to tell everyone about it, but in reality or when tested, you're probably very much how you've always been.

Family, children and having an admired home is important to you and being the matriarch even more so. You love being mothers and provide for your children brilliantly like a lioness but you don't like the attention being drawn away from you for too long and that might mean you'll choose not to have children at all. You are more practical then intellectual but can feel insecure or inadequate by this apparent shortfall and sometimes will attempt to overcompensate for this by trying to be someone you're really not.

Sex:

From the outside, Mountain Expressions may seem quite shy and retiring when it comes to sexual matters but actually you have a strong and powerful sex drive, you're just not that overt about it. You can be very sensitive and giving lovers, gentle too, but single-minded and tenacious in pursing your needs. If you are not in the mood but feel pushed against your will, you may well 'go through the motions' but it's more likely you will retreat into your cave to reflect and be on your own.

Love:

8 Expressions have rather fixed views on the respective roles in a relationship but both males and females will want to try to control their partners. The much needed balance though will be found in Yin partners and you need to recognise how important they are for your well-being and not to dismiss them so easily. You are much more sensitive than you let on and can be defensive if teased. Whilst not moralistic, you do tend to be monogamous and feel at ease in a stable one-to-one relationship.

9-Energy Natural Expressions:

8-1-3:

This is a powerful, single-minded triple Yang Expression that suits males well but is more 'complex' for females. Self-motivation, ambition, hard work and independence are going to be high on your agenda as is honesty, a strong sense of fair play and 'doing the right thing'. You hate to be held back and are very forward looking but tend to be narrow-minded and your impatience and sometimes quick temper can cause difficulties and be inconsiderate for others. Perhaps oddly given all that, you can come across as quite shy but that really is the face of your cautious and contemplative nature. You are pretty good at reading people and have a creative side that fuels original thought and ideas.

Sex, Love and Who Puts the Rubbish Out?

8-2-2:

You are a person who works hard and is always on the go. You have a lot of determination and self-motivation and an ambitious and adventurous spirit which is not always obvious as you can come across as rather reserved and conservative. You are engaging and charming and like to play a full part in social and family affairs as well as the wider community, where you are helpful, well organised and detail conscious. But you're really not that empathetic to other people's feelings, views or how they may want to do things and so at times you can be seen as being rather inconsiderate. You can be proud and obstinate but there is a lot of tender sensitivity under the surface too.

8-3-1:

Ambitious, assertive and adventurous, you're a confident, competitive and courageous individual who is strong-willed, single minded and with the energy and patience to overcome hard times and most difficulties. From the outside, you are likely to come across as cautious, shy and indecisive because underneath you're actually a sensitive and rather insecure person. You like to keep moving and hate to get stuck in one place for too long and have a powerful need for attention and recognition and even fame. Under pressure or if you feel threatened, you have the potential to be explosive and will defend yourself forcefully. As with all powerful Yang Expressions, connecting with stable Yin Expressions should help settle and ground you.

8-4-9:

From the outside, people may see rather a flamboyant and impulsive person and when they get to know you someone who appears calm, steady and straightforward; but actually underneath there are a lot of emotions swirling around which means decisions can be made rashly and just as rashly quickly changed again. You have strong determination and a single-mindedness for fair play coupled with a bright and insightful mind. You are your own greatest fan and can come across as quite arrogant at times, but you are kind and supportive within your social circle as long as things don't get too complicated or involved. You have natural leadership skills but your followers may have difficulty keeping up with your changed priorities.

8-5-8:

This is a very strong triple Yang Expression that wants to control and doesn't want to follow. You are driven, self-motivated and ambitious and have great strength and determination to overcome difficulties and challenges. You have lots of natural, grounded charm and can be a very likeable and attractive. But you can be stubborn, assertive and demanding and at times come across as quite hard and uncommunicative and will hold back your true feelings, although deep inside there is real warmth, passion and kindness. Your enthusiasm and ideas can be very inspiring but as a rule you prefer to be your own person free to move wherever you want to go. You need to be listened to, but you need to listen too, connecting naturally to stable Yin Expressions.

8-6-7:

Hard work is second nature to you and you use your strong-will, single-mindedness and energetic enthusiasm to achieve your goals. You come across as easy-going, fun and charming but you are also bold, ambitious, opinionated and very clear and precise (inflexible even) in what you want. The flip-side to your natural intuition is huge sensitivity, especially if you feel you are being criticised, although no one can criticise you better than yourself. You like new adventures and playing hard and you can be rather proud and difficult to get close to, but when you feel comfortable with someone you will show much tenderness and passion. You have an understated but classic style and like to achieve a certain degree of status within your work and social circles.

8-7-6:

Whilst there is a side to you that is most definitely charming, flexible and easy-going, you can also be direct, opinionated and dogmatic. Your admirable honesty can sometimes be too much and appear insensitive, which is ironic as your own high levels of sensitivity play a big part in your own life. You are very self-motivated, logical and have great organisational ability with a fine attention to detail. Couple this with your capacity for hard work and you have the ingredients for real leadership potential but as you hate displaying weakness, your natural assertiveness can easily turn to stubbornness and a reluctance to consider different approaches. You usually like to play a leading role in social and community life.

8-8-5:

This is a very Yang Expression which can be unyielding, single-minded, opinionated and controlling: attributes that are usually associated with the male psyche and so may cause difficulties for females. You have great drive and ambition to achieve your goals with a strong sense of justice and fair play which can tip over into obsession if left unchecked. You tend to be always active and looking for new adventures which can sometimes make it hard to stay satisfied. You can be charming, persuasive, witty and generous but with a degree of naivety that can be taken advantage of leaving you exposed and hurt. You are not always as outgoing and independent as you'd like to let on and need a stable Yin Expression to keep you grounded.

8-9-4:

This is an Expression that lends itself to creativity and specialist skills. You can be very single-minded and determined and appear completely comfortable and in charge of any situation. However, you are more than likely to be very moody and changeable allowing your emotions to get the better of you and so appearing both erratic and wilful. To the outside world, and leaving your self-consciousness to one side, you are likely to come across as confident, charming, entertaining and playful, which allows you to have the potential to be an inspirational and persuasive speaker. Whatever else, you are a proud, ambitious and driven individual, who whilst impulsive and indecisive at times, are essentially a kind, gentle and helpful person.

Fire Expressions

Number: 9 **Force:** Yin
Phase: Fire **Family Member:** Middle Daughter
Season: Summer **Time of Day:** Midday

What kind of person you are:
* Impulsive * Flamboyant * Extrovert * Vain * Self-conscious * Fickle * Sophisticated * Intelligent * Proud * Stormy * Successful * Self-confident * Farsighted * Determined * Short-tempered * Charming * Impatient * Sharp * Passionate

Relationships: 9 with 1: Compatible Opposites (Yin/Yang)
9 with 2: Parent-Child (Yin/Yin)
9 with 3: Child-Parent (Yin/Yang)
9 with 4: Child-Parent (Yin/Yin)
9 with 5: Parent-Child (Yin/Yang)
9 with 6: Passive Control (Yin/Yang)
9 with 7: Passive Inertia (Yin/Yin)
9 with 8: Parent-Child (Yin/Yang)
9 with 9: Friendship (Yin/Yin)

Generally Speaking

Fire is a Yin Expression, although it can easily be mistaken for Yang, because it's bright, beautiful, showy and successful. However, the centre of fire is empty and it needs external energy and fuel to survive and move - it can't do it by itself. So for you, it's the exterior that is important and that can come across as superficial and insincere. But you want to be the best and the brightest, where the spot light needs to shine firmly on you and then you will be funny, engaging, sparkling and charming: the star of the show! In essence your Natural Expression is laughter, smiles and being happy.

So yes, you're pleasure-seeking and self-indulgent but so too are you dramatic and theatrical. This will be exhausting and soon you will need to re-charge your batteries either by natural or non-natural means! Because you think you are the best and the brightest, it can lead to vanity and hubris and if you are not getting the attention and praise you think you should, to anxiety and deep insecurity.

Bright in both mind and personality, you make good leaders and at a senior level too but actually you work better as the deputy to a Yang Expression. Coming up with the 'idea' is not really your forte as you are better suited to the selling and marketing side and making it happen. Because you can be fickle and impulsive, you don't always consider properly the people around you and can flip between charm and anger in a flash of light. Roles where you can express yourself and be the centre of attention suit you well such as presenting, dancing or acting; or teaching as long as you can be tolerant and patient if your students can't keep up.

When you speak, your words can be inspiring and motivating in a fun and confident way, but look a little deeper and often there is not much substance to them. You're the master of the 'white lie' but with a poor short-term memory! And if the going gets tough, you probably won't see it through and will want to take your bright shining personality to the next situation or person.

Males:

Because this is a Yin Expression, it actually doesn't suit the male body that well and as a consequence it is categorised as a 'complex' Expression for a man. But it can be confusing, because a lot of the Fire characteristics can look 'right' for the extrovert male: charismatic, bright, fiery, explosive and these are qualities usually associated with Yang Expressions. All of which can give the impression of power, strength and leadership potential and inevitably you are likely to play to this, but the truth is it is mostly show, and things are all rather cooler and softer on the inside.

Nevertheless, it is the outside that is seen first and you are probably going to want to be seen and heard above all. This can manifest in many ways: flamboyant clothing, flashy cars, expensive jewellery and expressive language. So whilst some of this behaviour may seem inappropriate, it is your Natural Expression but so too is your still and calm centre. Learned Convention tells men to be the former and hide the latter. This is a mistake: both aspects are completely natural for you and should be equally expressed.

In a work environment, it's unlikely that you'll be writing the scripts or creating the ads or choreographing the steps, but you are going to want to be the celebrated actor, the star presenter or the leading dancer. And that is entirely right, for that is where your talents lie.

You can be a bit like the clichéd politician with an easy charm and winning charisma, who can deliver fine words but actually the words and the promises are all pretty empty. Despite that, you can engender a large and devoted following that will be loyal and faithful to the end. For those who believe they can see through the style, they will be disillusioned and even bitter at being misled and let down.

Females:

Fire Expressions are Yin and therefore this sits comfortably with the female body. Indeed, these women are overtly feminine in a bright and expressive way. You love being the centre of attention, drawing the focus of everyone around you, especially men, who can be dazzled and overwhelmed by the passion and excitement you publically exude. You want everyone to know that you are the main attraction, but when the party's over, you're likely to fall into an exhausted heap.

You can be demanding with a stubborn streak and in a dispute or argument can suddenly flare up and be quite aggressive but it will just as quickly die down. You can have a tendency to look down your nose at people and will choose not to hear or see things you don't want to. You can also be vulnerable to an addictive lifestyle especially if it involves sex, drugs and rock 'n' roll! If you lose focus or internalise too much, you can become irrational, highly anxious and depressed.

You love to dance, just for the sake of it and you are passionate, spirited, romantic and artistic. You are happy to give more than you receive and nowhere is that more evident than in motherhood. You love to give birth and love being a mother and will get very involved in the lives and wellbeing of your children.

Yang Expression plays a big part in your life: you are easily led and influenced by it, particularly Yang males, and you are likely to bend to their will. This is part of Yin's nature generally but you can be susceptible to being abused or corrupted and will end up believing whatever they say rather than what you know in your heart to be true. If you let go and connect with your Natural Expression, you are a beacon of clarity and truth – the most wonderful and inspiring bringer of light.

Sex:

Fire is the most passionate of all the Expressions and nowhere is that more evident than in the matter of sex. For many, you can come across as being an outrageous flirt but actually you are simply a naturally engaging and lively person, which will be very attractive to a potential partner. You enjoy sex being impulsive and spontaneous but your needs must be met and your desires and emotions fully satisfied. It's not one-way traffic by any means, for you use your instinctiveness and sensitivity to listen and respond to your partner's needs as well as expressing your own.

Love:

It's rare that you're without a partner and whilst you are loyal and loving (and expect the same in return), you will have no compunction to move on to someone new if your needs are not being met. You are romantic and emotional and will happily abandon yourself to your partner and as a rule will feel safer with someone who you think is more stable than you. This can make you 'clingy' and over-dependent and if there isn't a fairly constant stream of positive attention or if you're overly criticised, you will become introverted and depressed and lose a lot of self-confidence.

9-Energy Natural Expressions:

9-1-4:

You are probably going to come across as confident, bright, charismatic and intuitive. But equally you may seem to be rather vain, superior and impulsive. You have the potential to become an intelligent and inspiring leader but you can be obstinate, only hearing one side of the argument and dismissing the feelings and views of others. This can lead you to being isolated when times get difficult, but even though you're likely to retain your tenacious and assertive qualities, you'll probably become more cautious and wary. There is a strong independent streak about you and you can sometimes allow your pride and assertiveness to get the better of you. You are a bright and foresighted individual, who can be both brilliant and beguiling at the same time.

9-2-3:

This is an Expression about energy, enthusiasm, spontaneity and brilliance. You have great potential to set the world on fire with your creativity, clarity and capacity for hard work. You are very passionate and love to express yourself but the price can be costly on your highly sensitive and emotional state. For the truth is, you are very dependent, desperate almost, for the attention, praise and acknowledgment of others and if you feel it is not there, your confidence and well-being will be severely hit. You can make a good leader, albeit quite a conservative one, but you can be impatient, opinionated, temperamental and at times manipulative. You tend to devote a lot of time and energy to your social life and can be quite sentimental at times.

9-3-2:

From the outside, people are likely to see a conservative, reserved and somewhat proud person, but inside there is a lot of fire and passion which gives you great strength, intensity and a brilliant clarity of mind and purpose. You are also rather vain and pretty sensitive which can make you cautious and sometimes indecisive when taking decisions. When stressed, you can be explosive and express your opinions with a directness and force that may well be inappropriate. With a bright and flexible attitude, you are happy to work hard especially if it leads to a respected position or recognition. You can be tactful and diplomatic and be very detail conscious which can border on finicky as you are often seeking perfection.

9-4-1:

On the surface, you will probably appear as shy, reserved, cautious and actually quite vulnerable. You are likely to find it hard to express how you really feel, bottling up your sensitive emotions and feeding a real sense of insecurity. You're quite a perfectionist, so you like to take your time to make decisions, patiently applying logic and reason and a great deal of analysis in the process. You are open to being influenced but you are an influencer yourself and can show inspiring leadership qualities and commit to a great deal of hard work. You can be quite evasive at times, stubborn and impulsive too: and you do need continual praise and acknowledgment to assuage your sense of self-doubt.

9-5-9:

This is a bright and brilliant Expression and you are likely to be a person of intuition, vision and ideas. You can show real clarity when taking decisions or giving your opinion and will make them quickly and assertively but sometimes impatiently and impulsively. You can be very strong-willed, bold and demanding and always wanting to be in control. You can make an effective and confident, sometimes often overconfident, leader because there is a lot of pride and ego in the mix too. You can be quick to anger which can cause anxiety and resentment and demoralise your followers. You can be a bit flash and showy and over concerned by your appearance which borders on vanity. But you are really pretty sensitive and your confidence depends greatly on recognition and acknowledgement from others.

9-6-8:

There is a bright but reserved charisma about you; an intuitive and determined person who learns about life by actually living it, rather than by books or through other people. You want to be in control and have leadership responsibilities but your pride and ambition can sometimes border on pomposity. You are naturally intuitive with a very clear thought process and high levels of concentration. You can be inflexible and argumentative and will stubbornly fight your corner, although if things get too messy and difficult, you may well bale out. You are generally pretty easy going but you're actually quite a perfectionist, who is both cautious and detail-minded. You can be very self-critical and defensive, and take it badly if you feel you are being criticised.

9-7-7:

This is a triple Yin Expression, which sits comfortably with women, but is deemed more 'complex' for a man. Either way, you're very likely to be a charismatic person (which can teeter into vanity), who's easy-going, entertaining, funny and passionate. You're also pretty sensitive, touchy even, easily affected by what's going on around you and very defensive if you feel you're being criticised or mocked. Your excellent organising ability is strategic and shrewd and you have good attention to detail. If matters get difficult or unpleasant, you're unlikely to stick it for long and will seek an easier and more comfortable route. You take pride in how you look, you're generous to the people you like and can express yourself clearly and inspire those around you.

9-8-6:

Bright, ambitious and dignified, you are honest, sincere and direct; qualities which can take you to leadership roles, especially if that involves fairness, justice and human rights. You also have the potential to be vain, greedy, proud and overbearing. Whilst there is usually a hard exterior on show, there is a soft inside which can manifest as shyness with a desire to retreat into your cave. As with most 9 Expressions, there is great potential for clear and brilliant thinking and shining a light out of difficult situations but there is also an obstinate and self-indulgent streak. You like to have recognition for your achievements and what you do and count money and/or fame as an indicator of your success.

9-9-5:

You are likely to be entertaining, lively, friendly and generous with an effervescent and empathetic personality. This will make you attractive and socially popular but you can be quite impulsive and moody making it hard for people to know what to expect. You're also quite controlling, even domineering at times, and like to be the centre of attention. You can be very persuasive and convincing, although your words can actually be rather empty and short of real substance. You have a tendency to be a bit of a show-off and can be quite vain and pretentious with it, but that's usually hiding your sensitive and sometimes insecure side. You're good at simplifying complex issues and getting to the salient points but you do need constant reassurance that you're doing the right things.

CHAPTER 6

Relationships

Introduction

So at the risk of labouring the point, it needs to be said again that this is a philosophy where there is no such thing as a good or bad relationship or one that is better or worse than any other. You can describe a relationship as 'simple' or 'complex' or 'balanced' or 'unbalanced', just as long as that's not equated to being 'right' or 'wrong' or 'good' or 'bad'. Of course nothing is guaranteed and just because a relationship has a balanced fit, it doesn't mean it's going to 'work'. Also, please, please, please do not think for a moment that a successful and meaningful relationship has to look like something out of a Hollywood RomCom film. It doesn't. You can grow, give and receive love and support in any and every kind of relationship if you free your mind from hope, assumptions and expectations. Whilst your 9-Energy Natural Expressions will always stay the same, the relationship itself is never static; it's a dynamic, constantly changing phenomenon.

I also think it's a mistake to pre-judge the potential compatibility of a relationship based on your respective 9-Energy Natural Expressions. It is tempting, I'd admit, and in some eastern cultures it is exactly what happens, but personally I think going into any relationship where there is so much judgement and expectation before you even start puts too much pressure on each other. I suggest you just enjoy the journey and see where it goes and if things do start to get sticky or laboured, then have a look at your Expressions and how you relate to each other and that will very likely provide you with a road map to an easier terrain.

Simplistically speaking, your relationships tend to come in two forms: the ones you choose and the ones you don't (although some say that in nature there are no real choices!). The former are typically going to be people like your spouse, friends and chosen business partners and the latter your parents, siblings, children and existing work colleagues. Either way, it makes no difference, as this philosophy will provide insight and guidance in all your relationships past, present and future.

There are of course lots of factors affecting how two people relate to each other. In Part 1, I talked about our 9-Energy Natural Expression being how we were as a 4 year old child. Then as we get older, Learned Convention and 'life' starts to play an increasingly major factor in the way we behave and engage with others that we end up putting on so many layers that we become this great big Ego-Onion. The result is that for many of us, it's really two Ego-Onions having a relationship! There is nothing wrong with that as such, you can be two very content Ego-Onions, but because this is not your Natural Expression, harmony in the relationship is likely to be hard to maintain. This can lead to a sense of unease and then suffering and possibly illness. The truth is, you and your relationships will suffer if you continue to eschew your Natural Expression.

Let's now break down the factors affecting you and your relationships into their two states: Natural and Learned Convention.

Natural State

Our Natural State was determined at the moment of birth and is made up from your gender, whether you're Yin or Yang, your specific 9-Energy Natural Expression, which of the Elements you are and where you are positioned in the family. These topics were discussed in Chapter 3 in this part of the book and whilst it can all sound rather complicated and involved, it does provide all the insight we need when exploring the dynamics of our relationships in their Natural State.

Learned Convention

Learned Convention on the other hand is dominated by life's experiences, upbringing, peer groups, teachings, social culture and past relationships. These make up the layers encircling and often trying to overpower our core Natural Expression. Ultimately, it's impossible for that to succeed, but if given a free rein they will make a jolly good go of it and can cause much damage in the process. I often hear people say that it's our life's experiences that make us who we are, but what these experiences are doing is building up your Ego-Onion. And yes, this Ego-Onion is real, it is who you are, but it's not your Natural Expression – recognising the difference is fundamental to this philosophy.

So when it comes to relationships, if we engage predominately as our Ego-Onion, we are likely to continually repeat the same patterns of behaviour and 'mistakes' that have always dogged our relationships. If on the other hand, we set ourselves free and engage as our Natural Expression, then we can connect as nature intended – without having 'to do' anything or being someone we're not.

We will look at the influence of Learned Convention on our relationships a little later on but before then we need to look at how our relationships connect in their Natural State.

3 Types of Relationships

We relate to each other in three principle ways: as friends, as a parent to a child (and vice versa) or as partners. These can be taken literally of course but <u>all</u> your relationships will fall into one of these categories whether romantic, personal or professional. As always, nature is about balance and to achieve that we need to connect equally with each of the three relationships. It's like that three legged table I spoke about in Part 1 Chapter 5, but this time with each leg representing one of the three types of relationships. If the legs are even, it's stable and anything on top of it is likely to stay on but if any of the legs are of unequal length, they're not. This tells us that it is simply impossible for one person to tick all your relationship needs, and if you believe they can, your table will just end up having one very long leg - and try keeping anything on top of that for any length of time!

How we define these three types of relationships requires us to consider something called the 'Law of 5 Transformation' which basically tells us how everything connects with everything else in the Universe. This shows where each of the 9 Expressions sits within the 5 Elements and how they all relate to each other. It may look a bit complicated, but wow, is it packed with insight and power?!

```
         FIRE
          9

WOOD              EARTH
3,4                2,5,8


     WATER    METAL
       1       6,7
```

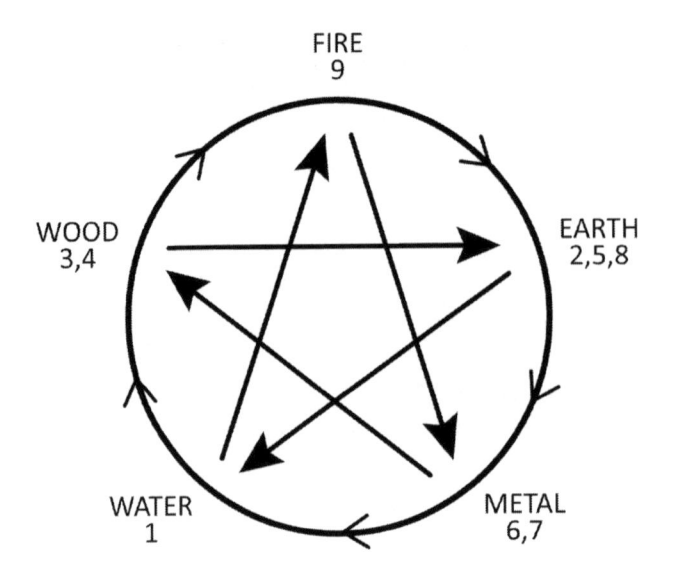

There are three forces at work here and their dynamic depends on the direction of the Energy arrows (clockwise around the circumference or internally) and where each of the Expressions (1 through to 9) sits within the different Elements (Fire, Earth, Metal, Water or Wood). Like Yin and Yang, the Elements maintain their harmony by mutual checks and balances and are continually moving and transforming.

As far as relationships are concerned, you and your partner's Expressions can either be within the same Element, the one adjacent or the one opposite. This then gives us our three types of relationships.

Friendship

If both your Expressions share the same Element, then this is a Friendship relationship or often called a Brother-Sister relationship. So for instance, if your Expression sits within the Earth Element you can have a friendship relationship with 2, 5 or 8. If, on the other hand, your Expression is a 1, you can only have a friendship relationship with another 1 because there are no other Expressions within the Water Element.

As would be expected, Friendship relationships are all about mutual understanding and compatibility. It is likely to be calm and easy-going with both being on the same wavelength most of the time. It's the sort of relationship where one person tends to finish the other person's sentences. So whilst there may not be much of an 'edge' there may not be much of a 'spark' either. This is particularly true if you both share the same Expression but much less so when there is a Yin Yang balance i.e. 3 (Yang) with 4 (Yin) in Wood, 6 (Yang) with 7 (Yin) in Metal or 2 (Yin) with either 5 (Yang) or 8 (Yang) in Earth.

Romantically, these are the relationships that typically last for life, indeed it is not untypical that when one dies, the other will die relatively soon after.

Parent - Child

These are the relationships where the Expression in one Element supports the Expression in the adjacent one, with the Energy arrows moving in a clockwise direction. Hence Fire supports Earth, which supports Metal, which supports Water, which supports Wood and which support Fire. The supportive direction is not all one way though, with about 20% of the support flowing back in the opposite direction. This type of relationship can be referred to as a Mother – Child, but whilst these are all symbols, I prefer the less specific term of Parent.

Like the Friendship relationship, this is regarded as a stable type but the support the Parent gives to the Child can be draining for the Parent and not always what's good for the Child, who may become too dependent.

Partners

The third type of relationship is Partners (or Opposites or Husband and Wife). Here we need to take note of the direction of the internal Energy arrows within the diagram. This can be a bit complicated but depending upon the direction of the arrows and the Yin Yang quality of the two respective Expressions, four types of Partner relationships are possible. Some of the terms I've used to describe them may seem a bit blunt, so don't let them become definitions, but opposites attract and as long as both partners accept their Natural Expression, turn away from their Ego-Onions and simply accept that this is how they connect in nature then harmony will follow.

Compatible Opposites

This is where the Energy arrow flows from Yang to Yin giving a balanced opposite. So these are 3 to 2; 6 to 4; 1 to 9. So whilst these are opposites, you are compatible and provide for a dynamic and often passionate relationship. Issues can arise if the male is Yin and thinks he should be Yang or when the Yang female plays at being Yin – both these scenarios should be avoided! Another issue is when the Yang becomes too dominating and/or the Yin becomes too yielding and this can lead to the Yang abusing the Yin with disastrous results for both.

Conflict Opposites

In these types of relationships, it is Yang on Yang i.e. 3 wanting to control 5 & 8; 5 & 8 wanting to control 1; 6 wanting to control 3. It's likely to be explosive and sparks are going to fly with neither of the Yang Expressions wanting to yield. It may be passionate but usually only for a short period of time before the conflicts start. It can 'work' if both parties have lots of space and whilst you are likely to believe that compromise is the key to long term success, the person who does most of the compromising (typically the female) could end up being increasingly resentful and their health badly affected.

Passive Control

In this case, we have Yin trying to control or dominate Yang and this will be found in 4 trying to control 5 & 8; 9 trying to control 6; 2 trying to control 1; 7 trying to control 3. The problem is that Yin can't control Yang and whilst it is slightly less of an issue if the Yin Expression is female, it can be a bigger problem if it is male and he is much older. This is because he may think that he should lead and take control of the relationship (and she might too), but this attempt at Passive Control by the Yin will damage both the Yin and the Yang Expressions, but mostly the Yin.

Passive Inertia

This is a Yin on Yin situation: 4 trying to control 2; 9 trying to control 7; 7 trying to control 4. With so much Yin around, it means the relationship is likely to stagnate with little movement or dynamism. To counter this, one of the Expressions (probably the 4, 9 or 7 and usually the man) will try to provide direction and leadership, but they actually won't be very good at it, or at least not for any length of time.

Sex, Love and Who Puts the Rubbish Out?

So having looked at the three types of relationships, we now need to consider some of the other Natural States that affect our relationships.

Yin and Yang

Of course, the whole of this book is really about the forces of Yin and Yang but we now need to look at this in relation to the genders and also the relative power of each of the Expressions.

Firstly the genders: it doesn't take much maths to work out that if there are two forces (Yin and Yang) and two genders (male and female), there have to be four 'States of Being' i.e. Yang males, Yang females, Yin males and Yin females.

Irrespective of your gender, nature says that Yang will lead, direct and set the boundaries of a relationship. They have no choice; and for their own wellbeing it is what they must do. Conversely, and for the good of their own health, Yin must yield and be led. As Yang is essentially male and Yin is female, those States of Being (i.e. Yang males and Yin females) are classed as 'simple' and their relationship will be deemed to be balanced. Whilst by contrast, Yang females and Yin males would be classed as 'complex' with their relationship being equally balanced.

Yang males and Yin females tend to see the demarcation of the sexes very clearly i.e. both are likely to accept that the male should lead and 'be men'. Indeed, the Yin female will probably only accept leadership from the male (and actually will be unable to discriminate between either Yang or Yin males) but will resist Yang females if they consider them to be a challenge for the attention of the male.

Out of the four States of Being, only the Yang male is probably living closest to their Natural Expression. This is because we live in a Yang dominated society where competiveness, winning and being hard are all deemed to be necessary for 'success'. They therefore fit in well, being the archetypical alpha-male, and will only really take leadership from a stronger Yang male.

Yin males on the other hand, may be seen as weak or poodle-like when they follow a Yang female but are usually more comfortable taking leadership from them rather than a Yang male. They are likely to hide their 'softness' by 'manning-up' and trying to be tough and hard.

As for Yang females, if they are being true to their Natural Expression, they are likely to be strong, dominant women, comfortable at leading both in their relationships and in their chosen place of work. No problem of course, but society can still consider that to be 'unfeminine' and in some cultures, it simply unacceptable or even illegal to take that sort of role. Yang women may then compromise their Yangness to 'fit in' and feel they should be more demure and girly.

And then there are the Yin females, who are the softest and gentlest of them all. But in the world today, being wallflowers or worse being 'trodden on' are not deemed as acceptable options. Instead, they'll often pretend to be way more assertive and hard than they really are and will end up probably just being passive aggressive.

Both Yang males and Yin females are likely to group together and will struggle to understand or 'see' the Yin male or the Yang female. But the Yin male and the Yang female will naturally connect, but may not quite understand why or how that is happening and may try to resist by being someone they are not.

In short, Yang has to look outward and connect with Yin and by doing so must listen and understand Yin. Then they can lead, as they are naturally supposed to do, without abusing the Yin. On the other hand, Yin has to look inwards and in effect do nothing; they won't find the answer by looking outside of themselves.

The other aspect that needs to be considered is the relative power of the Yin and Yang forces within the relationship. 3 Thunder is the most Yang and 7 Lake the most Yin. This is the order: 3-6-5-8-1-9-4-2-7. Thus in a male-female Conflict Opposites relationship if the male is 3 and the female 1, the female 1 may be more comfortable yielding to the male 3 and so a kind of wobbly balance may be possible. Similarly say in a Passive Inertia relationship, if the 9 is male and the 7 is female, a balance of sorts may be achieved.

Family Members

The final aspect of our Natural State we need to have a look at is where our Natural Expression sits within the family. Chapter 3 goes into this in more detail but by way of a recap this is it:

6 - Father
2 - Mother
3 - Eldest Son

4 - Eldest Daughter
1 - Middle Son
9 - Middle Daughter
8 - Youngest Son
7 - Youngest Daughter
5 - Seventh Child

The actual gender is not to be taken literally but rather as a representation of its quality or energy, with the 5 Expression sitting at the centre of the family and is sometimes referred to as the Seventh Child.

How the family members relate to each other and who is likely to lead or likely to yield is all taken into consideration when exploring the dynamics of a relationship, but it will be fairly subtle and doesn't carry the same weight as the other factors we have been considering.

So before we explore how we relate to each other in the Natural State, let's take a few moments to consider what happens when we identify with our mind instead of our Natural Expression and how that simply builds layer upon layer on our ever expanding Ego-Onion.

Now I'm the first to agree that it's all very well saying that to find relief and happiness all we need do is to simply set ourselves free and live our lives as our Natural Expression, but when the realities of the 'real world' get in the way all the time, that could well be unrealistic.

But what is this 'real world'? Is it what we've learnt from our parents, our peer groups or our partner? Is it from our experiences of the cruel knocks of life or failed relationships or events out of our control? Or is it from the media, holy books or our teachers? The list goes on and it seems inevitable that our actions, decisions and emotions are going to be influenced by what we have seen, heard, felt or done before. But this world is the world of your mind, the minds of the people around you and of those who seek to influence or rule over you. And these minds will change over time and due to circumstances, as will yours, and so this 'real world' is nothing but an illusion. The rules of Natural Expression are the rules of nature, and those are the ones that cannot change.

So on that note, let's now see how each Natural Expression relates to the other based upon the Transformation Diagram discussed earlier. It should be noted that primarily these have been written with a romantic relationship in mind but it doesn't take much to see how this can translate for personal and professional relationships as well.

1. Sea Expressions

Male to Female:

1 with 1:

Friendship: you will both need your independence and space and if that can be achieved you are likely to work well together and be a couple enjoying equal status. When you pool your resources you will make good progress but if one or the other is struggling, it will affect you both and you are likely to be better off tackling the issue alone rather than together. Difficulties may arise if one tries to control the other and this will typically be the man who is the stronger Yang force.

Who puts the rubbish out? You'll take turns.

1 with 2:

Passive Control: this is where the 2 Yin female will try to control the 1 Yang male which will simply annoy the male (assuming he takes much notice) and frustrate the female. The female will need to acquiesce to the male if this has a chance of being a close relationship. Whilst that can work as far as his Yang to her Yin, there is conflict because the Energy arrows are flowing from 2 Yin to 1 Yang. Her attempt at 'control' is therefore likely to be of a passive aggressive nature and trying to hold him back.

Who puts the rubbish out? He will, although she may keep pestering him to do it.

1 with 3:

Parent - Child: a 1 Yang male parent with a 3 Yang female child is likely to work better in business and friendship and in a literal parent-child sense, but it's not so smooth for romantic relationships. This is because the 3 Yang female will take the authority of the 1 Yang male only up to a point, but then is likely to 'rebel' when she wants to do her own thing and enact her own ideas. Rather than yield, the 1 Yang male is likely try to increase his attempt at control.

Sex, Love and Who Puts the Rubbish Out?

Who puts the rubbish out? He will, to begin with; then you'll fight over it.

1 with 4:

Parent - Child: this is a smooth combination for family, business, friendship and romantic relationships. The parent is 1 Yang and male, the child is 4 Yin and female, which means there is a natural leader and a natural follower at every level: parent to child, Yang to Yin and male to female. Where there may be issues is that the 1 Yang male may become too dominant and authoritative and not listen or try to understand the 4 Yin female. This potential abuse of the 4 Yin female will be very unhealthy for you both.

Who puts the rubbish out? He will, but may tell her to in order to make a point.

1 with 5:

Conflict Opposites: this is likely to make for a difficult relationship. The 1 Yang male with a 5 Yang female is potentially going to be explosive as neither will be able to yield or compromise, at least not for any length of time. There may be moments of great passion but it won't be long or take very much to set off the next conflict or argument. If possible, lots of space should be given (living apart for instance) and both need to respect the other's views and opinions, which may not be easy.

Who puts the rubbish out? You'll fight over it.

1 with 6:

Child - Parent: this is a 6 Yang female being the parent to the 1 Yang male child. In the friendship and family dynamic, this can work well and in business too. But romantically it may not be quite so easy, mainly because it is two Yang Expressions with the 6 Yang female being the parent. However, because the 1 Yang is very close, and can easily be mistaken for a Yin Expression, if he is happy to yield then this could work, especially if she is quite a bit older than him.

Who puts the rubbish out? She'll tell him to, but it may get messy.

1 with 7:

Child - Parent: here the 1 Yang male is the child to the 7 Yin female. You are likely to make for a very sociable couple and if you can pool your respective talents will make a powerful, maybe even a spiritual, combination. If the 7 Yin female is true to her Natural Expression, she will have an important, yet subtle influence on the 1 Yang male, guiding him to do the 'right' things, as far as she sees it! You should make good friends and business partners too, as this is a perfectly balanced 'simple' relationship.

Who puts the rubbish out? She'll suggest he does it; and he'll agree.

1 with 8:

Conflict Opposites: this is where the 8 Yang female will try to control the 1 Yang male and is unlikely to succeed, or at least not for very long. Conversely, the 1 Yang male will not see much movement (if any) from the 8 Yang female and will struggle to both understand and trust her. Your disputes and arguments might be fierce, although you are just as likely to completely ignore each other. There is no clear leader in this relationship.

Who puts the rubbish out? You'll fight over it.

1 with 9:

Compatible Opposites: this is a completely balanced partnership relationship with the 1 Yang male going towards the 9 Yin female. As you are complete opposites, you will very likely have pretty different views on life and how to live it, which may cause difficulties, as the 1 Yang male tends to be careful and understated whilst the 9 Yin female is impetuous and outspoken. But if you let yourselves go, forget about Learned Convention and live your Natural Expression, this is a complete YinYang fit.

Who puts the rubbish out? He will; no problem.

Female to Male:

1 with 1:

Friendship: you will both need your independence and space and if that can be achieved you are likely to work well together and be a couple enjoying equal status. When you pool your resources you will make good progress but if one or the other is struggling, it will affect you both and you are likely to be better off tackling the issue alone rather than together. Difficulties may arise if one tries to control the other and this will typically be the man who is the stronger Yang Expression.

Who puts the rubbish out? You'll take turns.

1 with 2:

Passive Control: this is where the 2 Yin male will try to control the 1 Yang female and because Learned Convention tells us the man usually leads the relationship, you both might try to comply. That will be a mistake because the best chance of success is if the 2 Yin male lets the 1 Yang female take the lead. He probably needs to take the back seat and not try to 'man up' even if the 1 Yang female suggests that he should. If you can both accept your own and each other's Natural Expression, there is a YinYang balance here but there will be difficulties.

Who puts the rubbish out? Both will think the man should; you'll both be wrong.

1 with 3:

Parent - Child: this is where the parent is a 1 Yang female and the child is a 3 Yang male. In the literal sense, this is where the ambitious parent pushes the child to be successful and whilst the child may eventually rebel, the 1 Yang female will understand and emphasise with the 3 Yang male's need for independence. In other types of relationships, this could be a challenging match with both trying to control the other and neither wanting to yield.

A lot of compromise is likely to be needed which long-term is probably unsustainable.

Who puts the rubbish out? She may tell him to, but it's likely to be a battle of wills (or won'ts).

1 with 4:

Parent - Child: here we have a 1 Yang female being the parent to a 4 Yin male. Both are 'complex' Expressions and are therefore balanced which potentially makes this is a smooth fit. The 4 Yin male needs to see that she is both Yang and his parent and therefore accept that she is going to be leading and setting the boundaries in the relationship. But she needs to listen and respect him and he will help ground her if she becomes too 'up in her head' or close minded.

Who puts the rubbish out? She will, but sometimes he wrongly thinks he should.

1 with 5:

Conflict Opposites: like all relationships of this type, this could be challenging. The 5 Yang male will want to control things and be at the centre of everything, whilst the 1 Yang female will also want to take up a leadership position. Something's got to give and the male will almost certainly want it to be the female! The ingredients are there for a very physical relationship but so are the fights for dominance. Space and time apart will be needed.

Who puts the rubbish out? You'll fight over it.

1 with 6:

Child - Parent: this is two Yang Expressions, but with the 6 Yang male being the parent, this can potentially be quite harmonious, although there's unlikely to be too many dull moments! In many ways, the leadership can be shared and certainly the big decisions will need to be agreed jointly. As you are both strong-willed, you will need to be singing from the same hymn sheet otherwise there may be deadlock and you will probably need to seek a third party to help you resolve the issue.

Who puts the rubbish out? He'll think it's his duty to, but she'll think that's nonsense.

1 with 7:

Child - Parent: this 'complex' relationship is totally balanced in that there is 1 Yang female with a 7 Yin male. However, because the male is in the parental position, he may well try to shield his Yin by being overly masculine and controlling. This will be a mistake because the female is much better suited to leading the relationship. If things are difficult with one, you may both go down and suffer equally, but there is great potential for a deeply spiritual relationship.

Who puts the rubbish out? He may think he should; she must put him straight.

1 with 8:

Conflict Opposites: in this relationship, the 8 Yang male will be in conflict with the 1 Yang female, both fighting for dominance and leadership. It's therefore more likely to be a difficult relationship with neither partner really being able to understand or empathise with the other. If you just want to have fun, then fun you will likely have, but anything more serious or contentious then sparks are likely to fly as compromise will be difficult and hard to sustain.

Who puts the rubbish out? You'll fight over it.

1 with 9:

Compatible Opposites: this is a balanced relationship, albeit a 'complex' one, with the 9 Yin male and the 1 Yang female. As in all of these types of relationships, the 9 Yin male must understand that she will need space and time away from him and will be the leader in the relationship. He will be more dependent but may hide that by being showy and extroverted. This is likely to be one of those 'opposites attract' relationships but has great potential to be a happy and harmonious one.

Who puts the rubbish out? She will; no problem.

Same Sex:

1 with 1:

Friendship: both will need your independence and space, but you will be very much on the same wavelength and be good friends easily being able to pick up your relationship if there is a long time apart. If one is struggling, the other will be supportive, but probably not that empathetic and the support is likely to be one-dimensional. That may be exactly what is wanted, but if it is not, you will need to seek help outside of the relationship.

Who puts the rubbish out? You'll share it.

1 with 2:

Passive Control: here the 2 Yin Expression is trying to control the 1 Yang and will most likely not succeed. If this is a male-on-male relationship, the 2 will probably try quite hard to lead and will find it very difficult to yield, although if he did things would be smoother. For females, the 1 Yang will probably just ignore the 2 Yin or be quite precise and demanding in what she wants. This will leave the 2 Yin female frustrated which may manifest as passive-aggressive behaviour. It's usually not a great match.

Who puts the rubbish out? The 1 Yang will, but the 2 Yin won't be impressed.

1 with 3:

Parent - Child: this is likely to be a harmonious relationship for either gender with lots of mutual understanding of each other's needs. In all the different types of relationships, personal, professional or romantic, it is the 1 Yang who will be the parental figure but more in a guidance sort of way

Sex, Love and Who Puts the Rubbish Out?

rather than trying to dominate. The 3 Yang will take everything 1 Yang can give, but will not be obliged to follow any of the paths suggested, which may ultimately drain and be despairing for the 1 Yang.

Who puts the rubbish out? The 1 Yang will tell the 3 Yang how to do it.

1 with 4:

Parent - Child: this is a smooth combination for family, business, friendship and romantic relationships. The parent is 1 Yang and the child is 4 Yin; so there is a natural leader and teacher and a natural follower and pupil. Where there may be issues is that the 1 Yang parent may become too dominant and authoritative and not listen or understand the 4 Yin's indecisiveness. Or the 4 Yin child will become too demanding and draining for the 1 Yang. Simply being aware of those potential scenarios will help.

Who puts the rubbish out? The 1 Yang will, but may tell the 4 Yin to just to make a point.

1 with 5:

Conflict Opposites: this is likely to be a pretty competitive relationship – in attracting attention at work to get a promotion, for a sexual partner or in the family. The 5 Yang will try to control and be at the centre of things but that's what the 1 Yang will want to do as well. You will be fighting for dominance with arguments and tempers flying. Your truces are likely to be short and uneasy and only for convenience in order to get what either of you want.

Who puts the rubbish out? You'll fight over it.

1 with 6:

Child - Parent: in business, this is a sort of relationship where the 6 Yang parent is the Chairman and the 1 Yang child is the Chief Exec. You will really understand each other and your respective roles will be well defined. Outsiders are likely to see a very united front in terms of direction and purpose but internally there may be differences of opinion which if large enough could have serious consequences, as neither of you are likely to back down easily.

Who puts the rubbish out? You both can, but the 6 Yang may want it done only its way.

1 with 7:

Child - Parent: this is a 7 Yin Expression being the parent to the 1 Yang child and is a totally balanced and compatible relationship. The 1 Yang child will expect the 7 Yin parent to always be there and be a sounding board for its thoughts and ideas and whilst it will often seek approval and reassurance, it is just as likely to do what it pleases anyway! As the majority of the support is from Yin to Yang, the 7 Yin can quickly become drained if the 1 Yang is particularly demanding.

Who puts the rubbish out? The 1 Yang will, and both will be happy with that.

1 with 8:

Conflict Opposites: this is where the 8 Yang is trying to control the 1 Yang, which will probably make for a very competitive relationship, with horns being locked at regular intervals as neither of you will want to give ground. However, if you pool your resources, huge amounts can be achieved, but with no one acting as a brake, you are just as likely to go off the road or spend so much time arguing, you don't even get started in the first place.

Who puts the rubbish out? You'll fight over it.

1 with 9:

Compatible Opposites: this is a totally balanced YinYang relationship. If you each live your life as your Natural Expression, this could be a harmonious and rewarding relationship. You would make excellent business partners with your respective strengths and weaknesses being perfectly balanced out. Whilst you both have leadership potential, the 9 Yin is actually better at being the deputy, which works well because the 1 Yang is a natural leader.

Who puts the rubbish out? The 1 Yang will; with the 9 Yin being an excellent No 2.

2. Earth Expressions

Male to Female:

2 with 1:

Passive Control: this is where the 2 Yin male will try to control the 1 Yang female and because Learned Convention tells us the man usually leads the relationship, you both might try to comply. That will be a mistake because the best chance of success is if the 2 Yin male lets the 1 Yang female take the lead. He probably needs to take the back seat and not try to 'man up' even if the 1 Yang female suggests that he should. If you can both accept your own and each other's Natural Expression, there is a YinYang balance here but there will be difficulties.

Who puts the rubbish out? Both will think he should; you'll both be wrong.

2 with 2:

Friendship: this is likely to be an easy-going, steady and conservative relationship. Your views on life and how to lead it will probably be pretty similar and you will be both very supportive of each other. As you are both Yin and with a tendency to be stubborn, there may not be much dynamism in the relationship and there is a risk of stagnation. The man will probably try to lead and exert more control, but it's not his natural way, and a connection to an external Yang Expression may be needed to provide direction for larger decisions.

Who puts the rubbish out? You'll take turns or do it together.

2 with 3:

Compatible Opposites: this is where two 'complex' Expressions (the 2 Yin male and the 3 Yang female) are perfectly balanced, although your respective Expressions have very little in common. The 2 Yin male is likely to be steady and conservative, whilst the 3 Yang female will be dynamic and creative. He may see her as being rash; she frustrated by his caution. The 2

Yin male must let the 3 Yang female lead but she must respect and listen to him, otherwise unnecessary difficulties will arise.

Who puts the rubbish out? She will, but she should listen to him on how to do it.

2 with 4:

Passive Inertia: this is a Partners' type relationship, but with two Yin Expressions there is likely to be a tendency towards stagnation with neither really getting as much out of the relationship as you would like. The 2 Yin male may well try to take leadership of the relationship but the 4 Yin female will have her own ideas (whilst changing then often!) and may find him too conservative. Your mutual frustration may manifest as squabbling and being critical of each other and if this becomes the norm, it may be difficult to resolve.

Who puts the rubbish out? If it gets done at all, he probably will, but you'll bicker over it.

2 with 5:

Friendship: there is likely to be a smooth connection here with the 'complex' Expressions of the 2 Yin male and 5 Yang female providing balance within a supportive, yet dynamic relationship. Both need to recognise that the 5 Yang female will be the controlling Expression, but the 2 Yin male may try to challenge that (openly or passively) which will likely have a negative effect on the relationship as she will struggle to yield, although she may believe that she is. But if both can 'see' the other, this has the making of a strong relationship.

Who puts the rubbish out? She will, and he won't really have a choice.

2 with 6:

Parent - Child: although these are 'complex' expressions (a 2 Yin male with a 6 Yang female) there is balance here and so this could be a really harmonious combination. You both must live your lives as your Natural

Expression rather than following 'the rules' of Learned Convention, which might be easier said than done! However tempting, he really shouldn't try to lead the relationship, but rather 'be there' for her being supportive, steady and strong, which will allow her to do the leading.

Who puts the rubbish out? She will, and he must let her.

2 with 7:

Parent - Child: here we have a 2 Yin male parent with a 7 female Yin child. In a romantic relationship, the 7 Yin female is likely to be flirty, somewhat naïve and actually rather insecure. The 2 Yin is male and in the parental role, which means he will probably try to steady and reassure her whilst at the same time being supportive and providing guidance. Romantically this may be hard to sustain, but may work better professionally if the 2 Yin male is able to take the lead.

Who puts the rubbish out? He probably will, although neither may be in a hurry to do it.

2 with 8:

Friendship: this is a friendship or brother-sister relationship with a 2 Yin male and an 8 Yang female. Your Expressions are deemed 'complex' but gives a YinYang balance and where the 2 Yin male's qualities of insight and dedication allow him to understand the 8 Yang female's stubbornness, tenacity and self-motivation. It means that she can feel safe and comfortable to be more open with her heart and mind. It is potentially a smooth match if he allows her to lead and set the boundaries.

Who puts the rubbish out? She will and it will feel right for both of you that she does.

2 with 9:

Child – Parent: here we have a 9 Yin female parent to a 2 Yin male child. There is a good mix of Expressions here with the 9 Yin female's flamboyance and showy qualities balanced with the more sober, steady and sincere

2 Yin male. However, it is the parent's role to be supportive and nurturing to the child, and in many ways, the roles here are reversed. This could be difficult in a romantic relationship if the respective boundaries are not defined and that may cause problems sustaining the relationship long term.

Who puts the rubbish out? No big issue here who does: probably best to toss a coin.

Female to Male:

2 with 1:

Passive Control: this is where the 2 Yin female will try to control the 1 Yang male which will simply annoy the male (assuming he takes much notice) and frustrate the female. The female will need to acquiesce to the male if this has a chance of being a close relationship. Whilst that can work as far as his Yang to her Yin, there is conflict because the Energy arrows are flowing from 2 Yin to 1 Yang. Her attempt at 'control' is therefore likely to be of a passive aggressive nature and trying to hold him back.

Who puts the rubbish out? He will, although she may keep pestering him to do it.

2 with 2:

Friendship: this is likely to be an easy-going, steady and conservative relationship. Your views on life and how to lead it will probably be pretty similar and you will be both very supportive of each other. As you are both Yin and with a tendency to be stubborn, there may not be much dynamism in the relationship and there is a risk of stagnation. The man will probably try to lead and exert more control, but it's not his natural way, and a connection to an external Yang Expression may be needed to provide direction for larger decisions.

Who puts the rubbish out? You'll take turns or do it together.

2 with 3:

Compatible Opposites: here there are two 'simple' Expressions (the 3 Yang male and the 2 Yin female) which are perfectly balanced, although your respective Expressions have very little in common, hence the complete YinYang fit. The 2 Yin female is likely to be steady and conservative, whilst the 3 Yang male will be dynamic and creative. She may see him as being rash, whilst he may be frustrated by her caution. The 3 Yang male will lead, but he must respect and listen to the 2 Yin female and not in any way abuse the Yin otherwise disaster will ensue.

Who puts the rubbish out? He will and that will be right for both of you.

2 with 4:

Passive Inertia: this is a Partners type relationship, but with two Yin Expressions there is likely to be a tendency towards stagnation with neither really getting as much out of the relationship as you would like. The 4 Yin male may try to lead the relationship, but the steadier and more conservative 2 Yin female will likely be rather bewildered by his sometimes flighty behaviour and insecurities. Your mutual frustration may manifest as bickering or just ignoring each other: better as friends than romantically.

Who puts the rubbish out? He will, but needs to be in the right frame of mind.

2 with 5:

Friendship: there is likely to be a smooth connection here with the 'simple' Expressions of the 5 Yang male and the 2 Yin female providing a total YinYang balance within a supportive yet dynamic relationship. The 5 Yang male will definitely be the controlling Expression, with the 2 Yin female being the 'power behind the throne'. She must yield and he must lead; but he must listen, respect and take notice of her needs and what she says. If he doesn't and ends up abusing her, it will be a disaster for both, but mainly for him.

Sex, Love and Who Puts the Rubbish Out?

Who puts the rubbish out? He definitely will; although you might publically say she does.

2 with 6:

Parent - Child: this is a perfectly balanced relationship with the parent being the 2 Yin female and the child being the 6 Yang male. He will lead the relationship and she will yield, but he will be demanding and doing the vast majority of the taking and probably not giving that much back in return. She will need to accept that but it will likely drain her and may make her feel isolated. He really needs her but may struggle to make her feel that.

Who puts the rubbish out? He will and both will be fine with that.

2 with 7:

Parent - Child: as a rule 2 Yin females are attracted to the classic alpha Yang male and so with 7 being the most Yin of all the Expressions, things are not off to a great start on the romantic front at least. But in a family or work environment this could work pretty well, as the 2 Yin female is naturally supportive and will have few issues with the 7 Yin male's cool and refined style. But with oceans of Yin between your two Expressions, the risk of inertia and stagnation is high.

Who puts the rubbish out? Neither most likely; but she will probably end up doing it.

2 with 8:

Friendship: here the 2 Yin female and the 8 Yang male should be a smooth match, as your Expressions are deemed as 'simple' and gives a YinYang balance. The 2 Yin female's qualities of insight and dedication allow her to understand the 8 Yang male's stubbornness, tenacity and self-motivation. Whilst he can feel secure and be more liable to open up with his heart and mind, there is the danger of the Yang abusing the Yin, which will be calamitous for both, but especially for him.

Who puts the rubbish out? He will and will do it very efficiently and that will suit you both.

2 with 9:

Child - Parent: here we have a 9 Yin male parent to a 2 Yin female child. Whilst there is a good mix of Expressions here with his flamboyance and showy qualities balanced with her more sober, steady and sincere approach, you both may be 'fooled' into thinking he is Yang. This illusion cannot be sustained and pretty soon she will probably be seeking something more solid and steady, which he will struggle to provide. In turn, he may find her too conservative and 'high maintenance' although probably he is the 'high maintenance' one.

Who puts the rubbish out? Probably she will, he will be too busy playing to the audience.

Same Sex:

2 with 1:

Passive Control: here the 2 Yin Expression is trying to control the 1 Yang and will most likely not succeed. If this is a male-on-male relationship, the 2 will probably try quite hard to lead and will find it very difficult to yield, although if he did things would be smoother. For females, the 1 Yang will probably just ignore the 2 Yin or be quite precise and demanding in what she wants. This will leave the 2 Yin female frustrated which may manifest as passive-aggressive behaviour. It's usually not a great match.

Who puts the rubbish out? The 1 Yang will, but the 2 Yin won't be impressed.

2 with 2:

Friendship: this is likely to be an easy-going, steady and conservative relationship. Your views on life and how to lead it will probably be pretty similar and you will both be very supportive of each other. As the two of you are Yin and with a tendency to be stubborn, there may not be much

Sex, Love and Who Puts the Rubbish Out?

dynamism in the relationship and there is a risk of stagnation. Particularly for romantic relationships, a connection to an external Yang Expression may be needed to provide direction for larger decisions.

Who puts the rubbish out? You'll take turns or do it together, but it may not happen at all.

2 with 3:

Compatible Opposites: here is a perfectly balanced YinYang connection, although your respective Expressions have very little in common. The 2 Yin is likely to be steady and conservative, whilst the 3 Yang will tend to be dynamic and creative. The 2 Yin may see the 3 Yang as being rash, whilst the 3 Yang may get frustrated by the 2 Yin's caution. The 3 Yang will lead, and the 2 Yin should yield, but the 3 Yang must respect and listen to the 2 Yin, otherwise the 3 Yang will become too ego-mind orientated.

Who puts the rubbish out? It will be the 3 Yang's responsibility and that's good for you both.

2 with 4:

Passive Inertia: this is a Partners type relationship, but with two Yin Expressions there is likely to be a tendency towards stagnation with neither really getting as much out of the relationship as you would like. Both Expressions tend to be followers rather than leaders, although the 4 Yin may try to lead the relationship, but the steadier and more conservative 2 Yin will likely be rather bewildered by the 4 Yin's sometimes flighty behaviour and insecurities. Your mutual frustration may manifest as bickering or just ignoring each other: better as friends than romantically.

Who puts the rubbish out? Either/or; if either can be bothered.

2 with 5:

Friendship: this is likely to be a harmonious relationship with a balanced YinYang connection laying the foundations for a supportive, yet dynamic partnership. The 5 Yang will definitely be the controlling Expression, with the 2 Yin being a powerful but more conservative force in the background. The 2 Yin must yield and the 5 Yang must lead; but the 5 Yang must listen, respect and take notice of the 2 Yin. If the 5 Yang doesn't, the balance will be lost and the relationship will suffer.

Who puts the rubbish out? Most definitely the 5 Yang, the 2 Yin has other things to do.

2 with 6:

Parent - Child: this is a perfectly balanced YinYang relationship, where the 6 Yang will lead the relationship and the 2 Yin will yield, but with the 6 Yang doing the vast majority of the taking and probably not giving that much back in return. The 2 Yin will need to accept that but it will be draining and is likely to make the 2 Yin feel isolated and even unwanted. The 6 Yang must connect and find balance with the 2 Yin and so must be very careful to respect and honour the 2 Yin.

Who puts the rubbish out? Most likely the 6 Yang and both should be fine with that.

2 with 7:

Parent - Child: these are the two most Yin of Expressions and with 2 Yin being the parent and the 7 Yin being the child, the 2 Yin is likely to provide most of the support and direction. This is the natural way of things and can work well and will provide satisfaction for each Expression. The 7 Yin though will not want to be suffocated or held back by the 2 Yin, with the 2 Yin being possibly overprotective and thinking that it knows best. The result can be stalemate and mutual frustration.

Who puts the rubbish out? The 2 Yin will, which may eventually get on the 7 Yin's nerves.

2 with 8:

Friendship: this is a friendship relationship with a naturally balanced YinYang match. The 2 Yin's qualities of insight and dedication allow it to understand the 8 Yang's stubbornness, tenacity and self-motivation. This will allow the 8 Yang to feel safe and be more liable to open up with its heart, mind and emotions, but there is always the danger of the 8 Yang abusing the 2 Yin, which will be calamitous for both, but especially for the 8 Yang.

Who puts the rubbish out? The 8 Yang will and will take its responsibilities seriously.

2 with 9:

Child - Parent: here we have a 9 Yin parent to a 2 Yin child. Whilst there is a good mix of Expressions here with the 9 Yin's flamboyance and showy qualities balanced with the more sober, steady and sincere 2 Yin, both may be fooled that the 9 Yin's behaviour is Yang. This cannot be sustained and pretty soon the 2 Yin will probably be seeking something more solid and steady which the other will struggle to provide. The 9 Yin may also find the 2 Yin being too conservative and 'high maintenance' although probably you can both fit into that category.

Who puts the rubbish out? Possibly the 2 Yin being the one which actually gets things done.

3. Thunder Expressions

Male to Female:

3 with 1:

Child - Parent: this is where the parent is a 1 Yang female and the child is a 3 Yang male. In the literal sense, this is where the ambitious parent pushes the child to be successful and whilst the child may eventually rebel, the 1 Yang female will understand and emphasise with the 3 Yang male's need for independence. In other types of relationships, this could be a challenging match with both trying to control the other and neither wanting to yield. A lot of compromise is likely to be needed which long-term is probably unsustainable.

Who puts the rubbish out? She may tell him to, but it's likely to be a battle of wills (or won'ts).

3 with 2:

Compatible Opposites: here there are two 'simple' Expressions (the 3 Yang male and the 2 Yin female) which are perfectly balanced, although your respective Expressions have very little in common, hence the complete YinYang fit. The 2 Yin female is likely to be steady and conservative, whilst the 3 Yang male will be dynamic and creative. She may see him as being rash, whilst he may be frustrated by her caution. The 3 Yang male will lead, but he must respect and listen to the 2 Yin female and not in any way abuse the Yin otherwise disaster will ensue.

Who puts the rubbish out? He will and that will be right for both of you.

3 with 3:

Friendship: with the two most Yang expressions together, there's likely to be no shortage of ideas or passion! There should also be a strong mutual understanding, although you may both choose to hide your very sensitive side from each other. You will both want to lead and if you can stay on the same page and communicate this will likely be a strong relationship. But there is a lot of potential for that not to be the case and impatience, frustration and explosive arguments (which should be quickly over) are likely to follow.

Who puts the rubbish out? Both will be comfortable doing it, but it may get competitive.

3 with 4:

Friendship: this is a totally balanced relationship with the 'simple' Expressions of the 3 Yang male and the 4 Yin female and this should be a smooth match if both can accept the other. The 3 Yang male is going to want to lead and set the boundaries and he will be very direct in how that is communicated. He will help her when she's being indecisive and she will try hard to fit in and understand his needs by using her gentle tenderness and intuition. He mustn't be dismissive of her as it will hurt both, but mainly him.

Who puts the rubbish out? He will and that's good for both of you.

3 with 5:

Conflict Opposites: this is likely to be a challenging relationship. The 3 Yang male will want to do things his way, lead the relationship and set the boundaries. The 5 Yang female will want to do the same, only her way! In the moments when you get along, there could be lots of passion and joy, but you are likely to need lots of space and time away from each other and a very defined set of 'rules' when you are together. If that doesn't happen, the break-ups will probably be frequent and messy.

Who puts the rubbish out? You'll probably end up throwing it at each other.

3 with 6:

Conflict Opposites: this is likely to be a challenging relationship because the 6 Yang female will want to control and lead the relationship but the 3 Yang male will have very different ideas. There's unlikely to be very much yielding, although she may be slightly more willing than him. Your compromises will have mixed success, but you will both need to recognise that you need time and space apart rather than being at loggerheads all the time, which will be utterly pointless and achieve nothing but mutual suffering.

Who puts the rubbish out? It will be a battle, and likely a pyrrhic victory for one or the other.

3 with 7:

Passive Control: this is where the 7 Yin female will try to control the 3 Yang male and will fail spectacularly. You both have 'simple' Expressions and there is a smooth YinYang fit, but unless the female realises that she will never really 'win' and must yield to the male, this is going to be a difficult relationship. The conflict here is that she thinks she should be doing a lot of the leading, or at least it should be shared, and because he doesn't, he will probably just be dismissive or much worse abusive.

Who puts the rubbish out? He will regardless of what she wants/does/asks.

3 with 8:

Conflict Opposites: as with most relationships of this type, it could be difficult to find long-term harmony. As the 3 Yang male will speak his mind freely regardless of the impact and the 8 Yang female will hold a grudge and struggle to see things differently from an entrenched position, the lines of communication are likely to be minimal and fraught. You are pretty opposite in your outlook and this will probably be a challenge for you both.

Who puts the rubbish out? You'll fight for it, and neither will win.

3 with 9:

Parent - Child: this is a perfectly balanced relationship with the 'simple' Expressions of the 3 Yang male and 9 Yin female. The 3 Yang male is also the 'parent' and will provide support and guidance which if sensitively given will be welcomed, but if perceived as instructions will not. He may regard her as 'high maintenance' and she will want to exert some control, but that may be in the passive aggressive sense if she thinks her wishes are being ignored or even abused. Overall this should be a smooth connection.

Who puts the rubbish out? He will, and both agree that he should.

Female to Male:

3 with 1:

Child - Parent: a 1 Yang male parent with a 3 Yang female child is likely to work better in business and friendship and in a literal parent-child sense, but it's not so smooth for romantic relationships. This is because the 3 Yang female will take the authority of the 1 Yang male only up to a point, but then is likely to 'rebel' when she wants to do her own thing and enact her own ideas. Rather than yield, the 1 Yang male is likely try to increase his attempt at control.

Who puts the rubbish out? He will, to begin with; then you'll fight over it.

3 with 2:

Compatible Opposites: this is where two 'complex' Expressions (the 2 Yin male and the 3 Yang female) are perfectly balanced, although your respective Expressions have very little in common. The 2 Yin male is likely to be steady and conservative, whilst the 3 Yang female will be dynamic and creative. He may see her as being rash; she frustrated by his caution. The 2 Yin male must let the 3 Yang female lead but she must respect and listen to him, otherwise unnecessary difficulties will arise.

Who puts the rubbish out? She will, but she should listen to him on how to do it.

3 with 3:

Friendship: with the two most Yang expressions together, there's likely to be no shortage of ideas or passion! There should also be a strong mutual understanding, although you may both choose to hide your very sensitive side from each other. You will both want to lead and if you can stay on the same page and communicate this will likely be a strong relationship. But there is a lot of potential for that not being the case and impatience, frustration and explosive arguments (which should be quickly over) are likely to follow.

Who puts the rubbish out? Both will be comfortable doing it, but it may get competitive.

3 with 4:

Friendship: this is a totally balanced relationship with the 'complex' Expressions of the 3 Yang female and the 4 Yin male. This should be a smooth match if both can accept the other: the female is likely to be very direct and will want to lead the relationship and set the boundaries and the man must let her and fit in. She will help him when he's being indecisive and he will understand her needs using his gentle tenderness and intuition. She mustn't be dismissive of him as it will hurt both, but mainly her.

Who puts the rubbish out? She will, but he may think he should. He'd be wrong.

3 with 5:

Conflict Opposites: this is likely to be a challenging relationship. The 3 Yang female will want to do things her way, lead the relationship and set the boundaries. The 5 Yang male will want to do the same, only more so! In the moments when you get along, there could be lots of passion and joy, but you are likely to need lots of space and time away from each other and a very defined set of 'rules' when you are together. If that doesn't happen, the break-ups will probably be frequent and messy.

Who puts the rubbish out? You'll probably end up throwing it at each other.

3 with 6:

Conflict Opposites: this is likely to be a challenging relationship because the 6 Yang male will want to lead and control the relationship and whilst the 3 Yang female may be willing to yield a little, it won't be by much, if at all. You will try to compromise with mixed success, but you will both need to recognise that you must have time and space apart rather than being at loggerheads all the time, which will be utterly pointless and achieve nothing but mutual suffering.

Who puts the rubbish out? It will be a battle, and likely a pyrrhic victory for one or the other.

3 with 7:

Passive Control: this is where the 7 Yin male will try to control the 3 Yang female and will fail spectacularly. You both have 'complex' Expressions and there is a smooth YinYang fit, but unless the male realises that he will never really 'win' and must yield to the female, this is going to be a difficult relationship. The conflict here is that he thinks he should be doing a lot of the leading, or at least it should be shared and because she doesn't, she will probably just be dismissive or even abusive.

Who puts the rubbish out? She will, and it really has to happen that way, whatever he says.

3 with 8:

Conflict Opposites: as with most relationships of this type, it could be difficult to find long-term harmony. As the 3 Yang female will speak her mind freely regardless of the impact and the 8 Yang male will hold a grudge and struggle to see things differently from an entrenched position, the lines of communication are likely to be minimal and fraught. You both can't lead and as you are pretty opposite in your outlook, this will probably be a challenge for you both.

Who puts the rubbish out? You'll fight for it, and neither will win.

3 with 9:

Parent - Child: this is a perfectly balanced relationship with the 'complex' Expressions of the 3 Yang female and 9 Yin male. She is also the 'parent' and will provide support and guidance which if sensitively given will be welcomed, but if perceived as instructions will not. She may regard him as 'highly sensitive' but he will want to exert some control and that may be in the passive aggressive sense, if he thinks his wishes are being ignored or even abused. But overall this should be a smooth connection.

Who puts the rubbish out? She will, and he needs to be OK with that.

Same Sex:

3 with 1:

Child - Parent: this is likely to be a harmonious relationship for either gender with lots of mutual understanding of each other's needs. In all the different types of relationships, personal, professional or romantic, it is the 1 Yang who will be the parental figure but more in a guidance sort of way rather than trying to dominate. The 3 Yang will take everything 1 Yang can give, but will not be obliged to follow any of the paths suggested, which may ultimately drain and be despairing for the 1 Yang.

Who puts the rubbish out? The 1 Yang will tell the 3 Yang how to do it.

3 with 2:

Compatible Opposites: here is a perfectly balanced YinYang connection, although your respective Expressions have very little in common. The 2 Yin is likely to be steady and conservative, whilst the 3 Yang will tend to be dynamic and creative. The 2 Yin may see the 3 Yang as being rash, whilst the 3 Yang may get frustrated by the 2 Yin's caution. The 3 Yang will lead, and the 2 Yin should yield, but the 3 Yang must respect and listen to the 2 Yin, otherwise the 3 Yang will become too ego-mind orientated.

Who puts the rubbish out? It will be the 3 Yang's responsibility and that's good for you both.

3 with 3:

Friendship: with the two most Yang expressions together, there's likely to be no shortage of ideas or passion! There should also be a strong mutual understanding, although you may choose to hide your very sensitive side from each other. You will both want to lead and if you can stay on the same page and communicate this will likely be a strong connection. But there is a lot of potential for that not being the case and impatience, frustration and explosive arguments (which should be quickly over) are likely to follow.

Who puts the rubbish out? Both will be comfortable doing it, but it may get competitive.

3 with 4:

Friendship: this is a balanced relationship with the 3 Yang and the 4 Yin. This should be a smooth match if both can accept the other: the 3 Yang will want to lead and set the boundaries and will be very direct in how that is communicated. That will help the 4 Yin when being indecisive and the 4 Yin will try hard to fit in and understand the 3 Yang's needs using gentle tenderness and intuition. The Yang mustn't be dismissive of the Yin, as it will hurt you both, but more so the Yang.

Who puts the rubbish out? The 3 Yang will and that's good for both of you.

3 with 5:

Conflict Opposites: this is likely to be a 'challenging' relationship. The 3 Yang will want to lead and set the boundaries. The 5 Yang will want to do the same, only more so! In the moments when you get along, there could be lots of passion and joy, but you are likely to need lots of space and time away from each other and a very defined set of 'rules' when you are together. If that doesn't happen the fall-outs will probably be frequent and messy.

Who puts the rubbish out? You'll probably end up throwing it at each other.

3 with 6:

Conflict Opposites: this is likely to be a challenging relationship because the 6 Yang will want to lead and control the relationship, but the 3 Yang will have very different ideas – there's unlikely to be very much real yielding. You will try to compromise with mixed success, but you must both recognise that you need time and space apart rather than being at loggerheads all the time, which will be utterly pointless and achieve nothing but mutual suffering.

Who puts the rubbish out? It will be a battle, and likely a pyrrhic victory for one or the other.

3 with 7:

Passive Control: this is where the 7 Yin will try to control the 3 Yang and will fail spectacularly. There is a smooth YinYang fit, but unless the 7 Yin realises that 'winning' is not really on the cards and must yield to the Yang, this is going to be a difficult relationship. The conflict here is that the 7 Yin thinks it should be doing a lot of the leading, or at least it should be shared, and because the 3 Yang doesn't, there is a possibility of the 7 Yin being dismissed or even abused.

Who puts the rubbish out? The 3 Yang will, and it has to be that way, whatever the 7 Yin says.

3 with 8:

Conflict Opposites: as with most relationships of this type, it could be difficult to find long-term harmony. As the 3 Yang will speak its mind freely regardless of the impact and the 8 Yang will hold a grudge and struggle to see things differently from an entrenched position, the lines of communication are likely to be minimal and fraught. You are pretty opposite in your outlook and this will probably be a challenge for you both.

Who puts the rubbish out? You'll fight for it, and neither will win.

3 with 9:

Parent - Child: this is a balanced YinYang relationship, where the 3 Yang is the 'parent' and will provide support and guidance to the 9 Yin, which if sensitively given will be welcomed, but if perceived as instructions will not. The 3 Yang may regard the 9 Yin as highly sensitive, but the 9 Yin will want to exert some control, but that may be in the passive aggressive sense, if it thinks its wishes are being ignored or even abused. Overall this should be a smooth connection.

Who puts the rubbish out? The 3 Yang will, and that will be fine for both.

4. Wind Expressions

Male to Female:

4 with 1:

Child - Parent: here we have a 1 Yang female being the parent to a 4 Yin male. Both are 'complex' Expressions and are therefore balanced which potentially makes this is a smooth fit. The 4 Yin male needs to see that she is both Yang and his parent and therefore accept that she is going to be leading and setting the boundaries in the relationship. But she needs to listen and respect him and he will help ground her if she becomes too 'up in her head' or close minded.

Who puts the rubbish out? She will, but sometimes he wrongly thinks he should.

4 with 2:

Passive Inertia: this is a Partners type relationship, but with two Yin Expressions there is likely to be a tendency towards stagnation with neither really getting as much out of the relationship as you would like. The 4 Yin male may try to lead the relationship, but the steadier and more conservative 2 Yin female will likely be rather bewildered by his sometimes flighty behaviour and insecurities. Your mutual frustration may manifest as bickering or just ignoring each other: better as friends than romantically.

Who puts the rubbish out? He will, but probably needs to be in the right frame of mind.

4 with 3:

Friendship: this is a totally balanced relationship with the 'complex' Expressions of the 3 Yang female and the 4 Yin male. This should be a smooth match if both can accept the other: the female is likely to be very direct and will want to lead the relationship and set the boundaries and the man must let her and fit in. She will help him when he's being indecisive and he will understand her needs using his gentle tenderness and intuition. She mustn't be dismissive of him as it will hurt both, but mainly her.

Who puts the rubbish out? She will, but he may think he should. He'd be wrong.

4 with 4:

Friendship: as with all friendship relationships, there is a lot of mutual support and understanding and particularly a tolerance towards the 4's changeable hopes, desires and moods. This is likely to be an easy-going relationship, but possibly too easy going, as both being Yin Expressions there is a real risk of stagnation which may result in a noncommittal union that doesn't really go anywhere. Both probably think they should lead the relationship with him shading it, but neither actually being particularly good at it: great for friends, not so romantically.

Who puts the rubbish out? He will, probably. Or maybe she will. Or perhaps neither.

4 with 5:

Passive Control: this is where the 4 Yin male will try to control the 5 Yang female and will fail miserably at his attempt. There is a complete, although 'complex', YinYang fit which has possibilities of working well, but only if the 4 Yin male lets the 5 Yang female lead and set the boundaries in the relationship. He will also need to understand and accept her need for space and time apart. That might sometimes be difficult, as energetically-wise he does want to control.

Who puts the rubbish out? She will, and that's the start and end of it.

4 with 6:

Compatible Opposites: this is a totally balanced YinYang fit with the 'complex' Expressions of the 4 Yin male and the 6 Yang female. If both can lead their lives as their Natural Expression and 'allow' their partner to do the same, this has great potential to work well. On the surface, there may be little obviously in common – you are opposites after all – but your opposites are totally compatible and complimentary. The 6 Yang female will lead the relationship and the 4 Yin male will always be there for her.

Who puts the rubbish out? She will, but she must listen if he suggests doing it differently.

4 with 7:

Passive Inertia: in this relationship, there are two Yin Expressions together and so whilst it's likely to be easy-going and probably fun and very sociable, there may not be much of a spark between you because without a Yang Expression providing direction, there is a real danger of stagnation. You both may also struggle to really 'get' the other and your mutual insecurities can mean a lot of dancing around subjects unsure of what the other is really meaning and then not trusting the response.

Who puts the rubbish out? He will, but he won't do it very well.

4 with 8:

Passive Control: typical of this relationship is the 4 Yin male trying to put his flag on top of the 8 Yang's mountain, and she will resist fiercely. Both will be rather bewildered by this, and the harder he tries to control, the worse it will become. But there is potential in this relationship because this is a 'complex' YinYang fit and if he lets go (he has to go first), she will do likewise. He must let her lead and allow her space and time away, and she must listen and respect him.

Who puts the rubbish out? Definitely her, not him – whatever he thinks.

4 with 9:

Parent - Child: whilst this is two Yin Expressions, there is potential for this combination because the 4 Yin male is in the parental position and his natural gentleness and easy-going manner compliments her flamboyance and keen mind. Both are likely to be OK that he tries to lead the relationship, but he may end up frustrating her when he is indecisive or conversely being stubborn and he may find her demands draining. Whilst there can be great passion here, ultimately though there may not be much substance in the relationship.

Who puts the rubbish out? He will want to, but may tire quite quickly.

Female to Male:

4 with 1:

Child - Parent: this is a smooth combination for family, business, friendship and romantic relationships. The parent is 1 Yang and male, the child is 4 Yin and female, which means there is a natural leader and a natural follower at every level: parent to child, Yang to Yin and male to female. Where there may be issues is that the 1 Yang male may become too dominant and authoritative and not listen or try to understand the 4 Yin female. This potential abuse of the 4 Yin female will be very unhealthy for you both.

Who puts the rubbish out? He will, but may tell her to in order to make a point.

4 with 2:

Passive Inertia: this is a Partners' type relationship, but with two Yin Expressions there is likely to be a tendency towards stagnation with neither really getting as much out of the relationship as you would like. The 2 Yin male may well try to take leadership of the relationship but the 4 Yin female will have her own ideas (whilst changing then often!) and may find him too conservative. Your mutual frustration may manifest as squabbling and being critical of each other and if this becomes the norm, it may be difficult to resolve.

Who puts the rubbish out? If it gets done at all, probably he will, but you'll bicker over it.

4 with 3:

Friendship: this is a totally balanced relationship with the 'simple' Expressions of the 3 Yang male and the 4 Yin female and this should be a smooth match if both can accept the other. The 3 Yang male is going to want to lead and set the boundaries and he will be very direct in how that is communicated. He will help her when she's being indecisive and she will try hard to fit in and understand his needs by using her gentle tenderness and intuition. He mustn't be dismissive of her as it will hurt both, but mainly him.

Who puts the rubbish out? He will and that's good for both of you.

4 with 4:

Friendship: as with all friendship relationships there is a lot of mutual support and understanding and particularly a tolerance towards the 4's changeable hopes, desires and moods. This is likely to be an easy-going relationship, but possibly too easy going, as both being Yin Expressions there is a real risk of stagnation, which may result in a noncommittal union that doesn't really go anywhere. Both probably think they should lead the relationship with him shading it, but neither actually being particularly good at it: great for friends, not so romantically.

Who puts the rubbish out? He will, probably. Or maybe she will. Or perhaps neither.

4 with 5:

Passive Control: this is where the 4 Yin female will try to control the 5 Yang male and have no chance. There is a complete and 'simple' YinYang fit which has possibilities of working well, but only if the 4 Yin female recognises that it is nature's way that the 5 Yang male must lead and set the boundaries in the relationship. She will also need to understand and accept his need for space and time apart but mustn't let him walk all over her.

Who puts the rubbish out? He will, and she won't get a look in despite trying.

4 with 6:

Compatible Opposites: this is a totally balanced YinYang fit with the 'simple' Expressions of the 4 Yin female and the 6 Yang male. If both can lead their lives as their Natural Expression and allow their partner to do the same, this has great potential to work well. On the surface, there may be little obviously in common – you are opposites after all – but your opposites are totally compatible and complimentary. The 6 Yang male will lead the relationship and the 4 Yin female will always be there for him.

Who puts the rubbish out? He will, and she will support him all the way.

4 with 7:

Passive Inertia: in this relationship, there are two Yin Expressions together and so whilst it's likely to be easy-going and probably fun and very sociable, there may not be much of a spark between you, because without a Yang Expression providing direction, there is a real danger of stagnation. Both may also struggle to really 'get' the other and your mutual insecurities can mean a lot of dancing around subjects unsure of what the other is really meaning and then not trusting the response.

Who puts the rubbish out? Toss up. Probably he will try, but both will prefer to party.

4 with 8:

Passive Control: here the 4 Yin female will try to exert some form of control over the 8 Yang male, but he'll just ignore it. This will frustrate her, and the harder she tries, the more distance will be created between you. There is however potential in this relationship because this is a 'simple' YinYang fit, which can work if she totally accepts his Expression and allows him to lead and to set the boundaries but without abuse from him.

Who puts the rubbish out? Definitely him: and she should just let him get on with it.

4 with 9:

Parent - Child: these are two Yin Expressions, with the parent being the 4 Yin female and the child being the 9 Yin male. This could lead to the 4 Yin female being drained or even exhausted by the demands of the flamboyant 9 Yin male. She will probably try to provide direction but he may well not listen. Both may think he should lead the relationship but really neither is going to be very good at it. Whilst there can be great passion here, ultimately though there may not be much substance in the relationship.

Who puts the rubbish out? She probably should; he will be too busy with other things.

Same Sex:

4 with 1:

Child - Parent: this is a smooth combination for family, business, friendship and romantic relationships. The parent is 1 Yang and the child is 4 Yin; so there is a natural leader and teacher and a natural follower and pupil. Where there may be issues is that the 1 Yang parent may become too dominant and authoritative and not listen or understand the 4 Yin's indecisiveness. Or the 4 Yin child will become too demanding and draining for the 1 Yang. Simply being aware of those potential scenarios will help.

Who puts the rubbish out? The 1 Yang will, but may tell the 4 Yin to just to make a point.

4 with 2:

Passive Inertia: this is a Partners type relationship, but with two Yin Expressions there is likely to be a tendency towards stagnation with neither really getting as much out of the relationship as you would like. Both Expressions tend to be followers rather than leaders, although the 4 Yin may try to lead the relationship, but the steadier and more conservative 2 Yin will likely be rather bewildered by the 4 Yin's sometimes flighty behaviour and insecurities. Your mutual frustration may manifest as bickering or just ignoring each other: better as friends than romantically.

Who puts the rubbish out? Either/or; if either can be bothered.

4 with 3:

Friendship: this is a balanced relationship with the 3 Yang and the 4 Yin. This should be a smooth match if both can accept the other: the 3 Yang will want to lead and set the boundaries and will be very direct in how that is communicated. That will help the 4 Yin when being indecisive and the 4 Yin will try hard to fit in and understand the 3 Yang's needs using gentle tenderness and intuition. The Yang mustn't be dismissive of the Yin, as it will hurt you both, but more so the Yang.

Who puts the rubbish out? The 3 Yang will and that's good for both of you.

4 with 4:

Friendship: as with all friendship relationships there is a lot of mutual support and understanding and particularly a tolerance towards the 4's changeable hopes, desires and moods. This is likely to be an easy-going relationship, but possibly too easy going, as both being Yin Expressions there is a real risk of stagnation which may result in a noncommittal union that doesn't really go anywhere. Both probably think they should lead the relationship with neither being particularly good at it: great for friends, not so romantically.

Who puts the rubbish out? Either/ or, if either or can be bothered.

4 with 5:

Passive Control: this is where the 4 Yin will try to control the 5 Yang and will fail miserably at the attempt. There is though a YinYang fit which has possibilities of working well, but only if the 4 Yin lets the 5 Yang lead and sets the boundaries in the relationship. The Yin will also need to understand and accept the Yang's need for space and time apart. That might be a tall order, as energetically-wise the Yin, in this type of relationship, does want to control.

Who puts the rubbish out? The 5 Yang will, and the 4 Yin won't get a look in.

4 with 6:

Compatible Opposites: this is a balanced YinYang fit with the 4 Yin and the 6 Yang. If both can lead their lives as their Natural Expression and allow the other to do the same, this has great potential to work well. On the surface, there may be little obviously in common – you are opposites after all – but your opposites are totally compatible and complimentary. The 6 Yang will lead the relationship and the 4 Yin will always be there supporting the Yang.

Who puts the rubbish out? The 6 Yang will, and both will be happy with that.

4 with 7:

Passive Inertia: in this relationship there are two Yin Expressions together and so whilst it's likely to be easy-going and probably fun and very sociable, there may not be much of a spark between you, because without a Yang Expression providing direction, there is a real danger of stagnation. Both may also struggle to really 'get' the other and your mutual insecurities can mean a lot of dancing around subjects unsure of what the other is really meaning and then not trusting the response.

Who puts the rubbish out? Toss up. Probably the 7 Yin will try, but both will prefer to party.

4 with 8:

Passive Control: here the 4 Yin will try to exert some form of control over the 8 Yang which will just be ignored. This will cause frustration and the harder the 4 Yin tries, the more distance will be created between you. There is however potential in this relationship because this is a YinYang fit, which can work if the 4 Yin totally accepts the 8 Yang's Expression allowing it to lead and to set the boundaries but without abuse from the 8 Yang.

Who puts the rubbish out? Definitely the 8 Yang and the 4 Yin should just let it get on with it.

4 with 9:

Parent - Child: these are two Yin Expressions, with the parent being the 4 Yin and the child being the 9 Yin. This could lead to the 4 Yin being drained or even exhausted by the demands of the flamboyant 9 Yin. The 4 Yin will probably try to provide direction but the 9 Yin may well not listen. Both may think that the 4 Yin should lead the relationship but really neither is going to be very good at it. Whilst there can be great passion here, ultimately though there may not be much substance in the relationship.

Who puts the rubbish out? The 4 Yin; the 9 Yin will be too busy with other things.

5. Earth Core Expressions

Male to Female:

5 with 1:

Conflict Opposites: like all relationships of this type, this could be challenging. The 5 Yang male will want to control things and be at the centre of everything, whilst the 1 Yang female will also want to take up a leadership position. Something's got to give and the male will almost certainly want it to be the female! The ingredients are there for a very physical relationship but so are the fights for dominance. Space and time apart will be needed.

Who puts the rubbish out? You'll fight over it.

5 with 2:

Friendship: there is likely to be a smooth connection here with the 'simple' Expressions of the 5 Yang male and the 2 Yin female providing a total YinYang balance within a supportive yet dynamic relationship. The 5 Yang male will definitely be the controlling Expression, with the 2 Yin female being the 'power behind the throne'. She must yield and he must lead; but he must listen, respect and take notice of her needs and what she says. If he doesn't and ends up abusing her, it will be a disaster for both, but mainly for him.

Who puts the rubbish out? He definitely will; although you might publically say she does.

5 with 3:

Conflict Opposites: this is likely to be a challenging relationship. The 3 Yang female will want to do things her way, lead the relationship and set the boundaries. The 5 Yang male will want to do the same, only more so! In the moments when you get along, there could be lots of passion and joy, but you are likely to need lots of space and time away from each other and a very defined set of 'rules' when you are together. If that doesn't happen, the break-ups will probably be frequent and messy.

Sex, Love and Who Puts the Rubbish Out?

Who puts the rubbish out? You'll probably end up throwing it at each other.

5 with 4:

Passive Control: this is where the 4 Yin female will try to control the 5 Yang male and have no chance. There is a complete and 'simple' YinYang fit which has possibilities of working well, but only if the 4 Yin female recognises that it is nature's way that the 5 Yang male must lead and set the boundaries in the relationship. She will also need to understand and accept his need for space and time apart but mustn't let him walk all over her.

Who puts the rubbish out? He will, and she won't get a look in despite trying.

5 with 5:

Friendship: whilst this is deemed a 'Friendship' relationship, you will need a well-defined common purpose and goals for this to be a harmonious one. The truth is, with two such strong Yang Expressions, there's probably not going to be much harmony, as both of you are stubborn and egotistical and will want to control and lead the other. You will probably create your much needed space and time apart by arguments and fights and whatever compromises you make, they probably won't hold for very long.

Who puts the rubbish out? Take a ringside seat and take cover.

5 with 6:

Parent - Child: this is a 6 Yang female child and 5 Yang male parent. This has the makings of the classic 'power couple'. Both are powerful Expressions and whilst the 5 Yang male will ultimately lead and control the relationship, he will recognise, like and respect the strength of the 6 Yang female. She will demonstrate calmness, and understand better than most his usually very positive, but sometimes turbulent nature. Pointing in the same direction, you will achieve much; if it goes wrong, it will go very wrong.

Who puts the rubbish out? He will, but both will know she can do it just as well.

5 with 7:

Parent - Child: this is a perfectly balanced 'simple' YinYang relationship. The 5 Yang male is the parent to the 7 Yin female and that makes for very clear lines of communication and control. She will be drawn to his alpha male attributes and he to her feminine style and individualism. She can be clever (even manipulative) at getting her own way by knowing when and how to negotiate with him and he will be very protective towards her, which may become stifling and controlling.

Who puts the rubbish out? He will; no question.

5 with 8:

Friendship: in this combination, the 8 Yang female will try to exert a degree of control by learning to temper her head-on approach and be more subtle and considered. But the communications between you are going to be challenging most of the time and there will always be an underlying conflict and battle in who will lead the relationship and sets the boundaries. Most likely, the 5 Yang male will want it his way, but it is unlikely the 8 Yang female will agree to that for long.

Who puts the rubbish out? He will, but it will become a battle of wills.

5 with 9:

Child - Parent: here we have a 9 Yin female being the parent to the 5 Yang male. This represents a balanced YinYang connection with two 'simple' Expressions and has the potential to being a harmonious relationship. This is because you both recognise the other's strengths are your weakness and vice versa. The 9 Yin female will be an intelligent, intuitive and inspiring partner and will support and give much to the 5 Yang male, liking his energy, discipline and personal control. Despite being the parent, she should take his leadership comfortably.

Who puts the rubbish out? She will tell him it's his responsibility – and she will be right.

Female to Male:

5 with 1:

Conflict Opposites: this is likely to make for a difficult relationship. The 1 Yang male with a 5 Yang female is potentially going to be explosive as neither will be able to yield or compromise, at least not for any length of time. There may be moments of great passion but it won't be long or take very much to set off the next conflict or argument. If possible, lots of space should be given (living apart for instance), and both need to respect the other's views and opinions, which may not be easy.

Who puts the rubbish out? You'll fight over it.

5 with 2:

Friendship: there is likely to be a smooth connection here with the 'complex' Expressions of the 2 Yin male and 5 Yang female providing balance within a supportive, yet dynamic relationship. Both need to recognise that the 5 Yang female will be the controlling Expression, but the 2 Yin male may try to challenge that (openly or passively) which will likely have a negative effect on the relationship as she will struggle to yield, although she may believe that she is. But if both can 'see' the other, this has the making of a strong relationship.

Who puts the rubbish out? She will, and he won't really have a choice.

5 with 3:

Conflict Opposites: this will probably be a challenging relationship. The 3 Yang male will want to do things his way, lead the relationship and set the boundaries. The 5 Yang female will want to do the same, only her way! In the moments when you get along, there could be lots of passion and joy, but you are likely to need lots of space and time away from each other and a very defined set of 'rules' when you are together. If that doesn't happen, the break-ups will probably be frequent and messy.

Who puts the rubbish out? You'll probably end up throwing it at each other.

5 with 4:

Passive Control: this is where the 4 Yin male will try to control the 5 Yang female and will fail miserably at his attempt. There is a complete, although 'complex', YinYang fit which has possibilities of working well, but only if the 4 Yin male lets the 5 Yang female lead and set the boundaries in the relationship. He will also need to understand and accept her need for space and time apart. That might sometimes be difficult, as energetically-wise he does want to control.

Who puts the rubbish out? She will, and that's the start and end of it.

5 with 5:

Friendship: whilst this is deemed a 'Friendship' relationship, you will need a well-defined common purpose and goals for this to be a harmonious one. The truth is, with two such strong Yang Expressions, there's probably not going to be much harmony, as both of you are stubborn and egotistical and will want to control and lead the other. You will probably create your much needed space and time apart by arguments and fights and whatever compromises you make, they probably won't hold for very long.

Who puts the rubbish out? Take a ringside seat and take cover.

5 with 6:

Parent - Child: this is a 5 Yang female parent with a 6 Yang male child. The female will want to control the relationship and that will be reinforced by being in the parental role. The male will be able to understand that because essentially he wants to do the same. You are likely to clash often, unless you are exactly on the same page, and in those times you will make for a very powerful couple. Ultimately, your two strong Yang Expressions are going to need lots of time and space apart, otherwise you will struggle to maintain any sense of harmony.

Who puts the rubbish out? You'll probably fight over it, or tell someone else to do it.

5 with 7:

Parent - Child: this is a perfectly balanced 'complex' YinYang relationship. The 5 Yang female is the parent to the 7 Yin male and that makes for very clear lines of communication and control. She will be drawn to his playful, warm and charming manner and he to her strong, determined and positive outlook. Both must 'let go', forget Learned Convention and be their Natural Expression. To some, the relationship may appear lop-sided, but that is how it has to be; if you pretend to be anything else, this will not work.

Who puts the rubbish out? She will; no question.

5 with 8:

Friendship: this is where both the 5 Yang female and 8 Yang male will want to lead and control the relationship. As friends or business partners this could work well, as long as you are equal, with the goals and what is to be achieved being clear and explicit. In the emotional whirlpool of romantic relationships, this is going to be a lot trickier. It's most likely going to be a battle of wills with neither able nor willing to yield in any meaningful sense.

Who puts the rubbish out? It will probably be a battle with neither prepared to give way.

5 with 9:

Child - Parent: here we have a 9 Yin male being the parent to the 5 Yang female. This represents a balanced YinYang connection with two 'complex' Expressions and has the potential to being a harmonious relationship. This is because you both recognise the other's strengths are your weakness and vice versa. The 9 Yin male will be an intelligent, intuitive and inspiring partner and will support and give much to the 5 Yang female, liking her energy, discipline and drive. He may be the parent, but he should take her leadership comfortably.

Who puts the rubbish out? She will, but he might every now and then.

Same Sex:

5 with 1:

Conflict Opposites: this is likely to be a pretty competitive relationship – in attracting attention at work to get a promotion, for a sexual partner or in the family. The 5 Yang will try to control and be at the centre of things but that's what the 1 Yang will want to do as well. You will be fighting for dominance with arguments and tempers flying. Your truces are likely to be short and uneasy and only for convenience in order to get what either of you want.

Who puts the rubbish out? You'll fight over it.

5 with 2:

Friendship: this is likely to be a harmonious relationship with a balanced YinYang connection laying the foundations for a supportive, yet dynamic partnership. The 5 Yang will definitely be the controlling Expression, with the 2 Yin being a powerful but more conservative force in the background. The 2 Yin must yield and the 5 Yang must lead; but the 5 Yang must listen, respect and take notice of the 2 Yin. If the 5 Yang doesn't, the balance will be lost and the relationship will suffer.

Who puts the rubbish out? Most definitely the 5 Yang, the 2 Yin has other things to do.

5 with 3:

Conflict Opposites: this is likely to be a 'challenging' relationship. The 3 Yang will want to lead and set the boundaries. The 5 Yang will want to do the same, only more so! In the moments when you get along, there could be lots of passion and joy, but you are likely to need lots of space and time away from each other and a very defined set of 'rules' when you are together. If that doesn't happen the fall-outs will probably be frequent and messy.

Who puts the rubbish out? You'll probably end up throwing it at each other.

5 with 4:

Passive Control: this is where the 4 Yin will try to control the 5 Yang and will fail miserably at the attempt. There is though a YinYang fit which has possibilities of working well, but only if the 4 Yin lets the 5 Yang lead and sets the boundaries in the relationship. The Yin will also need to understand and accept the Yang's need for space and time apart. That might be a tall order, as energetically-wise the Yin, in this type of relationship, does want to control.

Who puts the rubbish out? The 5 Yang will, and the 4 Yin won't get a look in.

5 with 5:

Friendship: whilst this is deemed a 'Friendship' relationship, you will need a well-defined common purpose and goals for this to be a harmonious one. The truth is, with two such strong Yang Expressions, there's probably not going to be much harmony, as both of you are stubborn and egotistical and will want to control and lead the other. You will probably create your much needed space and time apart by arguments and fights and whatever compromises you make, they probably won't hold for very long.

Who puts the rubbish out? Take a ringside seat and take cover.

5 with 6:

Parent - Child: this is a 5 Yang parent with a 6 Yang child. The 5 Yang will want to control and that will be reinforced by being in the parental role. The 6 Yang will be able to understand that because essentially it shares the same view. You are likely to clash often, unless you are exactly on the same page and in those cases you will make for a very powerful couple. Ultimately, you are two strong Yang Expressions and are going to need lots of space and time apart otherwise it will be a struggle to maintain any sense of harmony.

Who puts the rubbish out? You'll probably fight over it, or order someone else to do it.

5 with 7:

Parent - Child: this is a balanced YinYang relationship. The 5 Yang is the parent to the 7 Yin and that makes for very clear lines of communication and control. The 5 Yang will be drawn to the 7 Yin's playful, warm and charming manner and the 7 Yin to the 5 Yang's strength, determination and positive outlook. This has the potential to be a very harmonious relationship, just as long as the 5 Yang doesn't become too overbearing and controlling, which could actually happen quite easily.

Who puts the rubbish out? The 5 Yang will; no question.

5 with 8:

Friendship: in this combination, both the 5 Yang and 8 Yang will want to lead and control the relationship. As friends or business partners this could work well, as long as you are equal and the goals and what is to be achieved are clear and explicit. In the emotional whirlpool of romantic relationships, this is going to be a lot trickier. It's most likely going to be a battle of wills with neither able nor willing to yield in any meaningful sense.

Who puts the rubbish out? It will probably be a battle with neither prepared to yield.

5 with 9:

Child - Parent: here we have a 9 Yin being the parent to the 5 Yang. This represents a YinYang connection and has the potential to being a harmonious relationship. This is because you both recognise the other's strengths are your weakness and vice versa. The 9 Yin will be an intelligent, intuitive and inspiring partner and will support and give much to the 5 Yang, liking its energy, discipline and drive. The Yin should take the Yang's leadership comfortably.

Who puts the rubbish out? The 5 Yang will, but the 9 Yin might every now and then.

6. Sky Expressions

Male to Female:

6 with 1:

Parent - Child: this is two Yang Expressions, but with the 6 Yang male being the parent, this can potentially be quite harmonious, although there's unlikely to be too many dull moments! In many ways, the leadership can be shared and certainly the big decisions will need to be agreed jointly. As you are both strong-willed, you will need to be singing from the same hymn sheet otherwise there may be deadlock and you will probably need to seek a third party to help you resolve the issue.

Who puts the rubbish out? He'll think it's his duty to, but she'll think that's nonsense.

6 with 2:

Child - Parent: this is a perfectly balanced relationship with the parent being the 2 Yin female and the child being the 6 Yang male. He will lead the relationship and she will yield, but he will be demanding and doing the vast majority of the taking and probably not giving that much back in return. She will need to accept that but it will likely drain her and may make her feel isolated. He really needs her but may struggle to make her feel that.

Who puts the rubbish out? He will and both will be fine with that.

6 with 3:

Conflict Opposites: this is likely to be a challenging relationship because the 6 Yang male will want to lead and control the relationship and whilst the 3 Yang female may be willing to yield a little, it won't be by much, if at all. You will try to compromise with mixed success, but you will both need to recognise that you must have time and space apart rather than being at loggerheads all the time, which will be utterly pointless and achieve nothing but mutual suffering.

Who puts the rubbish out? It will be a battle, and likely a pyrrhic victory for one or the other.

6 with 4:

Compatible Opposites: this is a totally balanced YinYang fit with the 'simple' Expressions of the 4 Yin female and the 6 Yang male. If both can lead their lives as their Natural Expression and allow their partner to do the same, this has great potential to work well. On the surface, there may be little obviously in common – you are opposites after all – but your opposites are totally compatible and complimentary. The 6 Yang male will lead the relationship and the 4 Yin female will always be there for him.

Who puts the rubbish out? He will, and she will support him all the way.

6 with 5:

Child - Parent: this is a 5 Yang female parent with a 6 Yang male child. The female will want to control the relationship and that will be reinforced by being in the parental role. The male will be able to understand that because essentially he wants to do the same. You are likely to clash often, unless you are exactly on the same page, and in those times you will make for a very powerful couple. Ultimately, your two strong Yang Expressions are going to need lots of time and space apart, otherwise you will struggle to maintain any sense of harmony.

Who puts the rubbish out? You'll probably fight over it, or tell someone else to do it.

6 with 6:

Friendship: this is likely to be a relationship that should connect well, as you both have the same characteristics and therefore should be able to accept the other quite easily. Neither is likely to yield much, as you are both proud people who need to be respected. If one hurts the other, you must communicate calmly and rationally otherwise there will be the potential for misunderstandings which could lead to some big conflicts. You should make for a strong couple, as long as one doesn't try to dominate the other.

Who puts the rubbish out? There should be few problems with whoever does it.

6 with 7:

Friendship: here we have a perfectly balanced 'simple' YinYang connection with the 6 Yang male and the 7 Yin female. You should have similar natures which allows for mutual understanding and an easy-going manner together. The 6 Yang male will lead the relationship and the 7 Yin female must be comfortable to yield, but he may get frustrated by her hesitancy and she will be unhappy if he becomes too overbearing or dominating. Your roles and responsibilities are likely to be quite different in the relationship but you should complement each other.

Who puts the rubbish out? He will, always.

6 with 8:

Child - Parent: these are two Yang Expressions with the 6 Yang male being the child to the 8 Yang female parent. There is a mutual understanding here and for the majority of time you should be able to communicate well with each other. Because the 6 Yang male is a more natural leader, he is likely to take that role, whilst respecting and accepting the 8 Yang female's strength and determination. However, with two strong Yang Expressions, you will need space and time apart and to tackle the harder issues calmly and rationally, which might not always be easy.

Who puts the rubbish out? He should, but she can do it almost as well.

6 with 9:

Passive Control: here the 9 Yin female will try to control the 6 Yang male and will make a pretty poor go of it. This will frustrate the 9 Yin female who may become passively aggressive as a result. He's unlikely to take too much notice, will do his own thing anyway and probably not be that impressed by her tendency to be more show than substance. There is a strong YinYang connection, so if the 9 Yin female is prepared to yield, a degree of harmony can be achieved, but it probably won't be easy.

Sex, Love and Who Puts the Rubbish Out?

Who puts the rubbish out? He will, but she will try.

Female to Male:

6 with 1:

Parent - Child: this is a 6 Yang female being the parent to the 1 Yang male child. In the friendship and family dynamic, this can work well and in business too. But romantically it may not be quite so easy, mainly because it is two Yang Expressions with the 6 Yang female being the parent. However, because the 1 Yang is very close, and can easily be mistaken for a Yin force, if he is happy to yield then this could work, especially if she is quite a bit older than him.

Who puts the rubbish out? She'll tell him to, but it may get messy.

6 with 2:

Child - Parent: although these are 'complex' expressions (a 2 Yin male with a 6 Yang female) there is balance here and so this could be a really harmonious combination. You both must live your lives as your Natural Expression rather than following 'the rules' of Learned Convention, which might be easier said than done! However tempting, he really shouldn't try to lead the relationship, but rather 'be there' for her being supportive, steady and strong, which will allow her to do the leading.

Who puts the rubbish out? She will, and he must let her.

6 with 3:

Conflict Opposites: this is likely to be a challenging relationship because the 6 Yang female will want to control and lead the relationship but the 3 Yang male will have very different ideas. There's unlikely to be very much yielding, although she may be slightly more willing than him. Your compromises will have mixed success, but you will both need to recognise that you need time and space apart rather than being at loggerheads all the time, which will be utterly pointless and achieve nothing but mutual suffering.

Who puts the rubbish out? It will be a battle, and likely a pyrrhic victory for one or the other.

6 with 4:

Compatible Opposites: this is a totally balanced YinYang fit with the 'complex' Expressions of the 4 Yin male and the 6 Yang female. If both can lead their lives as their Natural Expression and 'allow' their partner to do the same, this has great potential to work well. On the surface, there may be little obviously in common – you are opposites after all – but your opposites are totally compatible and complimentary. The 6 Yang female will lead the relationship and the 4 Yin male will always be there for her.

Who puts the rubbish out? She will, but she must listen if he suggests doing it differently.

6 with 5:

Child - Parent: this is a 6 Yang female child and 5 Yang male parent. This has the makings of the classic 'power couple'. Both are powerful Expressions and whilst the 5 Yang male will ultimately lead and control the relationship, he will recognise, like and respect the strength of the 6 Yang female. She will demonstrate calmness, and understand better than most his usually very positive, but sometimes turbulent nature. Pointing in the same direction, you will achieve much; if it goes wrong, it will go very wrong.

Who puts the rubbish out? He will, but both will know she can do it just as well.

6 with 6:

Friendship: this is likely to be a relationship that should connect well, as you both have the same characteristics and therefore should be able to accept the other quite easily. Neither is likely to yield much, as you are both proud people who need to be respected. If one hurts the other, you must communicate calmly and rationally otherwise there will be the potential for misunderstandings which could lead to some big conflicts. You should make for a strong couple, as long as one doesn't try to dominate the other.

Sex, Love and Who Puts the Rubbish Out?

Who puts the rubbish out? There should be few problems with whoever does it.

6 with 7:

Friendship: here we have a balanced 'complex' YinYang connection with the 6 Yang female and the 7 Yin male. You should have similar natures which allows for mutual understanding and an easy-going manner together. The 6 Yang female will lead the relationship and the 7 Yin male must be comfortable to yield, but she may get frustrated by his hesitancy, and he in turn will be unhappy if she becomes too overbearing or dominating. Your roles and responsibilities are likely to be quite different in the relationship but you should complement each other.

Who puts the rubbish out? She will, always.

6 with 8:

Child - Parent: these are two Yang Expressions with the 6 Yang female being the child to the 8 Yang male parent. There is a mutual understanding here and for the majority of time you should be able to communicate well. Because the 6 Yang female is a more natural leader, she will probably want to take that role but he will likely have a different opinion! You are two strong Yang Expressions and you will need space and time apart and to tackle the harder issues calmly and rationally, which might not always be easy.

Who puts the rubbish out? It's likely to be a bit of a battle, but either can and will.

6 with 9:

Passive Control: here the 9 Yin male will try to control the 6 Yang female and will make a pretty poor go of it. This will bewilder and frustrate him who may become passively aggressive as a result. In turn, she may get hurt by his behaviour, but will end up doing her own thing anyway and probably not be that impressed by his tendency to be more show than substance. There is a 'complex' YinYang connection, so if he is prepared to yield, a degree of harmony can be achieved, but it probably won't be easy.

Who puts the rubbish out? She should, but he'll think he should.

Same Sex:

6 with 1:

Parent - Child: in business, this is a sort of relationship where the 6 Yang parent is the Chairman and the 1 Yang child is the Chief Exec. You will really understand each other and your respective roles will be well defined. Outsiders are likely to see a very united front in terms of direction and purpose but internally there may be differences of opinion which if large enough could have serious consequences, as neither of you are likely to back down easily.

Who puts the rubbish out? You both can, but the 6 Yang may want it done only its way.

6 with 2:

Child - Parent: this is a perfectly balanced YinYang relationship, where the 6 Yang will lead the relationship and the 2 Yin will yield, but with the 6 Yang doing the vast majority of the taking and probably not giving that much back in return. The 2 Yin will need to accept that but it will be draining and is likely to make the 2 Yin feel isolated and even unwanted. The 6 Yang must connect and find balance with the 2 Yin and so must be very careful to respect and honour the 2 Yin.

Who puts the rubbish out? Most likely the 6 Yang and both should be fine with that.

6 with 3:

Conflict Opposites: this is likely to be a challenging relationship because the 6 Yang will want to lead and control the relationship, but the 3 Yang will have very different ideas – there's unlikely to be very much real yielding. You will try to compromise with mixed success, but you must both recognise that you need time and space apart rather than being at loggerheads all the time which will be utterly pointless and achieve nothing but mutual suffering.

Sex, Love and Who Puts the Rubbish Out?

Who puts the rubbish out? It will be a battle, and likely a pyrrhic victory for one or the other.

6 with 4:

Compatible Opposites: this is a balanced YinYang fit with the 4 Yin and the 6 Yang. If both can lead their lives as their Natural Expression and allow the other to do the same, this has great potential to work well. On the surface, there may be little obviously in common – you are opposites after all – but your opposites are totally compatible and complimentary. The 6 Yang will lead the relationship and the 4 Yin will always be there supporting the Yang.

Who puts the rubbish out? The 6 Yang will, and both will be happy with that.

6 with 5:

Child - Parent: this is a 5 Yang parent with a 6 Yang child. The 5 Yang will want to control and that will be reinforced by being in the parental role. The 6 Yang will be able to understand that because essentially it shares the same view. You are likely to clash often, unless you are exactly on the same page and in those cases you will make for a very powerful couple. Ultimately, you are two strong Yang Expressions and are going to need lots of space and time apart otherwise it will be a struggle to maintain any sense of harmony.

Who puts the rubbish out? You'll probably fight over it, or order someone else to do it.

6 with 6:

Friendship: this is likely to be a relationship that should connect well, as you both have the same characteristics and therefore should be able to accept the other quite easily. Neither is likely to yield much, as you are both proud people who need to be respected. If one hurts the other, you must communicate calmly and rationally otherwise there will be the potential for misunderstandings which could lead to some big conflicts. You should make for a strong couple, as long as one doesn't try to dominate the other.

Who puts the rubbish out? There should be few problems with whoever does it.

6 with 7:

Friendship: here we have a balanced YinYang connection with the 6 Yang and the 7 Yin. You should have similar natures which allows for mutual understanding and an easy-going manner together. The 6 Yang will lead the relationship and the 7 Yin must be comfortable to yield. The 6 Yang may get frustrated by the 7 Yin's hesitancy, who in turn will be unhappy if the 6 Yang becomes too overbearing or dominating. Your roles and responsibilities are likely to be quite different in the relationship but you should complement each other.

Who puts the rubbish out? The 6 Yang will, always.

6 with 8:

Child - Parent: these are two Yang Expressions with the 6 Yang being the child to the 8 Yang parent. There is a mutual understanding here and for the majority of time you should be able to communicate well. Because the 6 Yang is a more natural leader, that Expression will probably want to take that role, but the 8 Yang will likely have a different opinion! These are two strong Yang Expressions and you will need space and time apart and to tackle the harder issues calmly and rationally, which might not always be easy.

Who puts the rubbish out? It's likely to be a bit of a battle, but either can.

6 with 9:

Passive Control: here the 9 Yin will try to control the 6 Yang and will make a pretty poor go of it. This will bewilder and frustrate the 9 Yin who may become passively aggressive as a result. The 6 Yang may get hurt by this behaviour, but will end up doing its own thing anyway and probably not be that impressed by the 9 Yin's tendency to be more show than substance. There is a YinYang connection, so if the 9 Yin is prepared to yield, a degree of harmony can be achieved, but it probably won't be easy.

Who puts the rubbish out? The 6 Yang will, but the 9 Yin may think it should.

7. Lake Expressions

Male to Female:

7 with 1:

Parent - Child: this 'complex' relationship is totally balanced in that there is 1 Yang female with a 7 Yin male. However, because the male is in the parental position, he may well try to shield his Yin by being overly masculine and controlling. This will be a mistake because the female is much better suited to leading the relationship. If things are difficult with one, you may both go down and suffer equally, but there is great potential for a deeply spiritual relationship.

Who puts the rubbish out? He may think he should; she must put him straight.

7 with 2:

Child - Parent: as a rule 2 Yin females are attracted to the classic alpha Yang male and so with 7 being the most Yin of all the Expressions, things are not off to a great start on the romantic front at least. But in a family or work environment this could work pretty well, as the 2 Yin female is naturally supportive and will have few issues with the 7 Yin male's cool and refined style. But with oceans of Yin between your two Expressions, the risk of inertia and stagnation is high.

Who puts the rubbish out? Neither most likely; but she will probably end up doing it.

7 with 3:

Passive Control: this is where the 7 Yin male will try to control the 3 Yang female and will fail spectacularly. You both have 'complex' Expressions and there is a smooth YinYang fit, but unless the male realises that he will never really 'win' and must yield to the female, this is going to be a difficult relationship. The conflict here is that he thinks he should be doing a lot of the leading, or at least it should be shared and because she doesn't, she will probably just be dismissive or even abusive.

Who puts the rubbish out? She will, and it really has to happen that way, whatever he says.

7 with 4:

Passive Inertia: in this relationship, there are two Yin Expressions together and so whilst it's likely to be easy-going and probably fun and very sociable, there may not be much of a spark between you, because without a Yang Expression providing direction, there is a real danger of stagnation. Both may also struggle to really 'get' the other and your mutual insecurities can mean a lot of dancing around subjects unsure of what the other is really meaning and then not trusting the response.

Who puts the rubbish out? Toss up. Probably he will try, but both will prefer to party.

7 with 5:

Child - Parent: this is a perfectly balanced 'complex' YinYang relationship. The 5 Yang female is the parent to the 7 Yin male and that makes for very clear lines of communication and control. She will be drawn to his playful, warm and charming manner and he to her strong, determined and positive outlook. Both must 'let go', forget Learned Convention and be their Natural Expression. To some, the relationship may appear lop-sided, but that is how it has to be; if you pretend to be anything else, this will not work.

Who puts the rubbish out? She will; no question.

7 with 6:

Friendship: here we have a balanced 'complex' YinYang connection with the 6 Yang female and the 7 Yin male. You should have similar natures which allows for mutual understanding and an easy-going manner together. The 6 Yang female will lead the relationship and the 7 Yin male must be comfortable to yield, but she may get frustrated by his hesitancy, and he in turn will be unhappy if she becomes too overbearing or dominating. Your roles and responsibilities are likely to be quite different in the relationship but you should complement each other.

Who puts the rubbish out? She will, always.

7 with 7:

Friendship: 7 is the most Yin of the Expressions, and so here we will find lots of mutual understanding and a similar outlook on life, but possibly not much passion and dynamism. Even though this is a Friendship relationship, you are likely to keep things from one another and be rather cautious and calculating about revealing your true feelings. If the relationship has any control, it is more probable to come from the male, but both will be drawn to Yang Expressions which will likely have a major impact on your relationship.

Who puts the rubbish out? It's a good question; it's unlikely either of you will be that bothered.

7 with 8:

Child - Parent: this is a perfectly balanced 'complex' YinYang relationship and has the potential to make a harmonious partnership with a lot of mutual respect and admiration. Whilst the 8 Yang female will definitely need to lead the relationship, there is much give-and-take, and there is balance in that the 7 Yin male will be gentle on the outside but strong on the inside; and the 8 Yang female who can have a hard and tough exterior but is actually very soft deep down.

Who puts the rubbish out? It will be part of her responsibilities: he will have others.

7 with 9:

Passive Inertia: this is where the 9 Yin female will try to control the 7 Yin male and really won't be very good at it, as it's not really her natural way. You both like to have an expressive even flamboyant lifestyle and are drawn to the same sorts of things. So in the early days, the relationship looks well-set, but as time goes on the differences between you will become more apparent. She will think he's all talk and no substance, and he will think she's vain and superior: neither is likely to concede much ground.

Who puts the rubbish out? 50/50: but maybe more her than him – just.

Female to Male:

7 with 1:

Parent - Child: here the 1 Yang male is the child to the 7 Yin female. You are likely to make for a very sociable couple and if you can pool your respective talents will make a powerful, maybe even a spiritual, combination. If the 7 Yin female is true to her Natural Expression, she will have an important, yet subtle influence on the 1 Yang male, guiding him to do the 'right' things, as far as she sees it! You should make good friends and business partners too, as this is a perfectly balanced 'simple' relationship.

Who puts the rubbish out? She'll suggest he does it; and he'll agree.

7 with 2:

Child - Parent: here we have a 2 Yin male parent with a 7 female Yin child. In a romantic relationship, the 7 Yin female is likely to be flirty, somewhat naïve and actually rather insecure. The 2 Yin is male and in the parental role, which means he will probably try to steady and reassure her whilst at the same time being supportive and providing guidance. Romantically this may be hard to sustain, but may work better professionally if the 2 Yin male is able to take the lead.

Who puts the rubbish out? He probably will, although neither may be in a hurry to do it.

7 with 3:

Passive Control: this is where the 7 Yin female will try to control the 3 Yang male and will fail spectacularly. You both have 'simple' Expressions and there is a smooth YinYang fit, but unless the female realises that she will never really 'win' and must yield to the male, this is going to be a difficult relationship. The conflict here is that she thinks she should be doing a lot of the leading, or at least it should be shared, and because he doesn't, he will probably just be dismissive or much worse abusive.

Who puts the rubbish out? He will regardless of what she wants/does/asks.

7 with 4:

Passive Inertia: in this relationship, there are two Yin Expressions together and so whilst it's likely to be easy-going and probably fun and very sociable, there may not be much of a spark between you because without a Yang Expression providing direction, there is a real danger of stagnation. You both may also struggle to really 'get' the other and your mutual insecurities can mean a lot of dancing around subjects unsure of what the other is really meaning and then not trusting the response.

Who puts the rubbish out? He will, but he won't do it very well.

7 with 5:

Child - Parent: this is a perfectly balanced 'simple' YinYang relationship. The 5 Yang male is the parent to the 7 Yin female and that makes for very clear lines of communication and control. She will be drawn to his alpha male attributes and he to her feminine style and individualism. She can be clever (even manipulative) at getting her own way by knowing when and how to negotiate with him and he will be very protective towards her, which may become stifling and controlling.

Who puts the rubbish out? He will; no question.

7 with 6:

Friendship: here we have a perfectly balanced 'simple' YinYang connection with the 6 Yang male and the 7 Yin female. You should have similar natures which allows for mutual understanding and an easy-going manner together. The 6 Yang male will lead the relationship and the 7 Yin female must be comfortable to yield, but he may get frustrated by her hesitancy and she will be unhappy if he becomes too overbearing or dominating. Your roles and responsibilities are likely to be quite different in the relationship but you should complement each other.

Who puts the rubbish out? He will, always.

7 with 7:

Friendship: 7 is the most Yin of the Expressions, and so here we will find lots of mutual understanding and a similar outlook on life, but possibly not much passion and dynamism. Even though this is a Friendship relationship, you are likely to keep things from one another and be rather cautious and calculating about revealing your true feelings. If the relationship has any control, it is more probable to come from the male, but both will be drawn to Yang Expressions which will likely have a major impact on your relationship.

Who puts the rubbish out? It's a good question; it's unlikely either of you will be that bothered.

7 with 8:

Child - Parent: this is a perfectly balanced 'simple' YinYang relationship and has the potential to make a harmonious partnership with lots of mutual respect and admiration. The 8 Yang male will definitely lead the relationship, but there is much give-and-take, and there is balance in that the 7 Yin female will be gentle on the outside but strong on the inside; and the 8 Yang male who can have a hard and tough exterior but is actually pretty soft deep down. If he becomes too controlling, he may well end up abusing her, and that will be a calamity for both, but mainly for him.

Who puts the rubbish out? He will; she will be doing other things.

7 with 9:

Passive Inertia: this is where the 9 Yin male will try to control the 7 Yin female and will make an OK job of it but it's not his natural way. You both like to have an expressive even flamboyant lifestyle and are drawn to the same sorts of things. So in the early days, the relationship looks well-set, but as time goes on the differences between you will become more apparent. He will think she's all talk and no substance; and she thinks he's vain and superior and will be unimpressed by his attempts at leadership: concessions are likely to be rare.

Who puts the rubbish out? He will and will want full marks for his style.

Same Sex:

7 with 1:

Parent - Child: this is a 7 Yin Expression being the parent to the 1 Yang child and is a totally balanced and compatible relationship. The 1 Yang child will expect the 7 Yin parent to always be there and be a sounding board for its thoughts and ideas and whilst it will often seek approval and reassurance, it is just as likely to do what it pleases anyway! As the majority of the support is from Yin to Yang, the 7 Yin can quickly become drained if the 1 Yang is particularly demanding.

Who puts the rubbish out? The 1 Yang will, and both will be happy with that.

7 with 2:

Child - Parent: these are the two most Yin of Expressions and with 2 Yin being the parent, and the 7 Yin being the child, the 2 Yin is likely to provide most of the support and direction. This is the natural way of things and can work well and will provide satisfaction for each Expression. The 7 Yin though will not want to be suffocated or held back by the 2 Yin, with the 2 Yin being possibly overprotective and thinking that it knows best. The result can be stalemate and mutual frustration.

Who puts the rubbish out? The 2 Yin will, which may eventually get on the 7 Yin's nerves.

7 with 3:

Passive Control: this is where the 7 Yin will try to control the 3 Yang and will fail spectacularly. There is a smooth YinYang fit, but unless the 7 Yin realises that 'winning' is not really on the cards and must yield to the Yang, this is going to be a difficult relationship. The conflict here is that the 7 Yin thinks it should be doing a lot of the leading, or at least it should be shared, and because the 3 Yang doesn't, there is a possibility of the 7 Yin being dismissed or even abused.

Who puts the rubbish out? The 3 Yang will, and it has to be that way, whatever the 7 Yin says.

7 with 4:

Passive Inertia: in this relationship there are two Yin Expressions together and so whilst it's likely to be easy-going and probably fun and very sociable, there may not be much of a spark between you, because without a Yang Expression providing direction, there is a real danger of stagnation. Both may also struggle to really 'get' the other and your mutual insecurities can mean a lot of dancing around subjects unsure of what the other is really meaning and then not trusting the response.

Who puts the rubbish out? Toss up. Probably the 7 Yin will try, but both will prefer to party.

7 with 5:

Child - Parent: this is a balanced YinYang relationship. The 5 Yang is the parent to the 7 Yin and that makes for very clear lines of communication and control. The 5 Yang will be drawn to the 7 Yin's playful, warm and charming manner and the 7 Yin to the 5 Yang's strength, determination and positive outlook. This has the potential to be a very harmonious relationship, just as long as the 5 Yang doesn't become too overbearing and controlling, which could actually happen quite easily.

Who puts the rubbish out? The 5 Yang will; no question.

7 with 6:

Friendship: here we have a balanced YinYang connection with the 6 Yang and the 7 Yin. You should have similar natures which allows for mutual understanding and an easy-going manner together. The 6 Yang will lead the relationship and the 7 Yin must be comfortable to yield. The 6 Yang may get frustrated by the 7 Yin's hesitancy, who in turn will be unhappy if the 6 Yang becomes too overbearing or dominating. Your roles and responsibilities are likely to be quite different in the relationship but you should complement each other.

Who puts the rubbish out? The 6 Yang will, always.

7 with 7:

Friendship: 7 is the most Yin of the Expressions, and so here we will find lots of mutual understanding and a similar outlook on life, but possibly not much passion and dynamism. Even though this is a Friendship relationship, you are likely to keep things from one another and be rather cautious and calculating about revealing your true feelings. Both of you will be drawn to Yang Expressions which will likely have a major impact on your relationship.

Who puts the rubbish out? It's a good question; it's unlikely either of you will be that bothered.

7 with 8:

Child - Parent: this is a balanced YinYang relationship and has the potential to make a harmonious partnership with a lot of mutual respect and admiration. The 8 Yang will definitely lead the relationship, but there is much give-and-take, and there is balance in that the 7 Yin will be gentle on the outside but strong on the inside; and the 8 Yang who can have a hard and tough exterior but is actually soft deep down. The 8 Yang may become too controlling and end up abusing the 7 Yin, and that will be a calamity for both, but mainly for the 8 Yang.

Who puts the rubbish out? The 8 Yang will; the 7 Yin will be doing other things.

7 with 9:

Passive Inertia: this is where the 9 Yin will try to control the 7 Yin and won't be very good at it. You both like to have an expressive even flamboyant lifestyle and are drawn to the same sorts of things. So in the early days the relationship looks well-set but as time goes on the differences between the two of you become more apparent. The 9 Yin will think the 7 Yin is all talk and no substance and the 7 Yin will think the 9 Yin's vain and superior and be unimpressed by its attempts at leadership: neither is likely to concede much ground.

Who puts the rubbish out? 50/50: but maybe more the 9 Yin – just.

8. Mountain Expressions

Male to Female:

8 with 1:

Conflict Opposites: in this relationship the 8 Yang male will be in conflict with the 1 Yang female, both fighting for dominance and leadership. It's therefore more likely to be a difficult relationship with neither partner really being able to understand or empathise with the other. If you just want to have fun, then fun you will likely have, but anything more serious or contentious then sparks are likely to fly as compromise will be difficult and hard to sustain.

Who puts the rubbish out? You'll fight over it.

8 with 2:

Friendship: here the 2 Yin female and the 8 Yang male should be a smooth match, as your Expressions are deemed as 'simple' and gives a YinYang balance. The 2 Yin female's qualities of insight and dedication allow her to understand the 8 Yang male's stubbornness, tenacity and self-motivation. Whilst he can feel secure and be more liable to open up with his heart and mind, there is the danger of the Yang abusing the Yin, which will be calamitous for both, but especially for him.

Who puts the rubbish out? He will and will do it very efficiently and that will suit you both.

8 with 3:

Conflict Opposites: as with most relationships of this type, it could be difficult to find long-term harmony. As the 3 Yang female will speak her mind freely regardless of the impact and the 8 Yang male will hold a grudge and struggle to see things differently from an entrenched position, the lines of communication are likely to be minimal and fraught. You both can't lead and as you are pretty opposite in your outlook, this will probably be a challenge for you both.

Who puts the rubbish out? You'll fight for it, and neither will win.

8 with 4:

Passive Control: here the 4 Yin female will try to exert some form of control over the 8 Yang male, but he'll just ignore it. This will frustrate her, and the harder she tries, the more distance will be created between you. There is however potential in this relationship because this is a 'simple' YinYang fit, which can work if she totally accepts his Expression and allows him to lead and to set the boundaries but without abuse from him.

Who puts the rubbish out? Definitely him: and she should just let him get on with it.

8 with 5:

Friendship: this is where both the 5 Yang female and 8 Yang male will want to lead and control the relationship. As friends or business partners this could work well, as long as you are equal, with the goals and what is to be achieved being clear and explicit. In the emotional whirlpool of romantic relationships, this is going to be a lot trickier. It's most likely going to be a battle of wills with neither able nor willing to yield in any meaningful sense.

Who puts the rubbish out? It will probably be a battle with neither prepared to give way.

8 with 6:

Parent - Child: these are two Yang Expressions with the 6 Yang female being the child to the 8 Yang male parent. There is a mutual understanding here and for the majority of the time you should be able to communicate well. Because the 6 Yang female is a more natural leader, she will probably want to take that role but he will likely have a different opinion! You are two strong Yang Expressions and you will need space and time apart and to tackle the harder issues calmly and rationally, which might not always be easy.

Who puts the rubbish out? It's likely to be a bit of a battle, but either can and will.

8 with 7:

Parent - Child: this is a perfectly balanced 'simple' YinYang relationship and has the potential to make a harmonious partnership with lots of mutual respect and admiration. The 8 Yang male will definitely lead the relationship, but there is much give-and-take, and there is balance in that the 7 Yin female will be gentle on the outside but strong on the inside; and the 8 Yang male who can have a hard and tough exterior but is actually pretty soft deep down. If he becomes too controlling, he may well end up abusing her, and that will be a calamity for both, but mainly for him.

Who puts the rubbish out? He will; she will be doing other things.

8 with 8:

Friendship: whilst this is a Friendship relationship with the mutual understanding of similar people, there is actually not a lot of trust here. This is because in this case, the 8's tendency towards stubbornness, jealously and self-indulgence is reinforced rather than dissipated and if these cannot be controlled by both partners, this is likely to be a challenging relationship. Both will want to lead and set the boundaries and although she may yield a little, it probably can't be sustained for long.

Who puts the rubbish out? You'll most likely argue over it.

8 with 9:

Child - Parent: this has the potential to work well, with the 9 Yin female being the parent to the 8 Yang male child, making for a 'simple' YinYang match. You will want to help each other and there is a lot of mutual respect for what the other can bring to the relationship with your respective 'weaknesses' being balanced by the other's 'strengths'. He will inevitably lead the relationship, but must be careful not to be too demanding and her not to be too giving.

Who puts the rubbish out? He will, and will be good at it.

Female to Male:

8 with 1:

Conflict Opposites: this is where the 8 Yang female will try to control the 1 Yang male and is unlikely to succeed, or at least not for very long. Conversely, the 1 Yang male will not see much movement (if any) from the 8 Yang female and will struggle to both understand and trust her. Your disputes and arguments might be fierce, although you are just as likely to completely ignore each other. There is no clear leader in this relationship.

Who puts the rubbish out? You'll fight over it.

8 with 2:

Friendship: this is a friendship or brother-sister relationship with a 2 Yin male and an 8 Yang female. Your Expressions are deemed 'complex' but gives a YinYang balance and where the 2 Yin male's qualities of insight and dedication allow him to understand the 8 Yang female's stubbornness, tenacity and self-motivation. It means that she can feel safe and comfortable to be more open with her heart and mind. It is potentially a smooth match if he allows her to lead and set the boundaries.

Who puts the rubbish out? She will and it will feel right for both of you that she does.

8 with 3:

Conflict Opposites: as with most relationships of this type, it could be difficult to find long-term harmony. As the 3 Yang male will speak his mind freely regardless of the impact and the 8 Yang female will hold a grudge and struggle to see things differently from an entrenched position, the lines of communication are likely to be minimal and fraught. You are pretty opposite in your outlook and this will probably be a challenge for you both.

Who puts the rubbish out? You'll fight for it, and neither will win.

8 with 4:

Passive Control: typical of this relationship is the 4 Yin male trying to put his flag on top of the 8 Yang's mountain, and she will resist fiercely. Both will be rather bewildered by this, and the harder he tries to control, the worse it will become. But there is potential in this relationship because this is a 'complex' YinYang fit and if he lets go (he has to go first), she will do likewise. He must let her lead and allow her space and time away, and she must listen and respect him.

Who puts the rubbish out? Definitely her, not him – whatever he thinks.

8 with 5:

Friendship: in this combination, the 8 Yang female will try to exert a degree of control by learning to temper her head-on approach and be more subtle and considered. But the communications between you are going to be challenging most of the time and there will always be an underlying conflict and battle in who will lead the relationship and sets the boundaries. Most likely, the 5 Yang male will want it his way, but it is unlikely the 8 Yang female will agree to that for long.

Who puts the rubbish out? He will, but it will become a battle of wills.

8 with 6:

Parent - Child: these are two Yang Expressions with the 6 Yang male being the child to the 8 Yang female parent. There is a mutual understanding here and for the majority of time you should be able to communicate well with each other. Because the 6 Yang male is a more natural leader, he is likely to take that role, whilst respecting and accepting the 8 Yang female's strength and determination. However, with two strong Yang Expressions, you will need space and time apart and to tackle the harder issues calmly and rationally, which might not always be easy.

Who puts the rubbish out? He should, but she can do it almost as well.

8 with 7:

Parent - Child: this is a perfectly balanced 'complex' YinYang relationship and has the potential to make a harmonious partnership with a lot of mutual respect and admiration. Whilst the 8 Yang female will definitely need to lead the relationship, there is much give-and-take, and there is balance in that the 7 Yin male will be gentle on the outside but strong on the inside; and the 8 Yang female who can have a hard and tough exterior but is actually very soft deep down.

Who puts the rubbish out? It will be part of her responsibilities: he will have others.

8 with 8:

Friendship: whilst this is a Friendship relationship with the mutual understanding of similar people, there is actually not a lot of trust here. This is because in this case, the 8's tendency towards stubbornness, jealously and self-indulgence is reinforced rather than dissipated and if these cannot be controlled by both partners, this is likely to be a challenging relationship. Both will want to lead and set the boundaries and although she may yield a little, it probably can't be sustained for long.

Who puts the rubbish out? You'll most likely argue over it.

8 with 9:

Child - Parent: this has the potential to work well, with the 9 Yin male being the parent to the 8 Yang female child, making for a 'complex' YinYang match. You will want to help each other and there is a lot of mutual respect for what the other can bring to the relationship with your respective 'weaknesses' being balanced by the other's 'strengths'. She will inevitably lead the relationship, but must be careful not to be too demanding and him not to be too giving.

Who puts the rubbish out? She will, and will be good at it.

Same Sex:

8 with 1:

Conflict Opposites: this is where the 8 Yang is trying to control the 1 Yang, which will probably make for a very competitive relationship, with horns being locked at regular intervals as neither of you will want to give ground. However, if you pool your resources, huge amounts can be achieved, but with no one acting as a brake, you are just as likely to go off the road or spend so much time arguing, you don't even get started in the first place.

Who puts the rubbish out? You'll fight over it.

8 with 2:

Friendship: this is a Friendship relationship with a naturally balanced YinYang match. The 2 Yin's qualities of insight and dedication allow it to understand the 8 Yang's stubbornness, tenacity and self-motivation. This will allow the 8 Yang to feel safe and be more liable to open up with its heart, mind and emotions, but there is always the danger of the 8 Yang abusing the 2 Yin, which will be calamitous for both, but especially for the 8 Yang.

Who puts the rubbish out? The 8 Yang will and will take its responsibilities seriously.

8 with 3:

Conflict Opposites: as with most relationships of this type, it could be difficult to find long-term harmony. As the 3 Yang will speak its mind freely regardless of the impact and the 8 Yang will hold a grudge and struggle to see things differently from an entrenched position, the lines of communication are likely to be minimal and fraught. You are pretty opposite in your outlook and this will probably be a challenge for you both.

Who puts the rubbish out? You'll fight for it, and neither will win.

8 with 4:

Passive Control: here the 4 Yin will try to exert some form of control over the 8 Yang which will just be ignored. This will cause frustration and the harder the 4 Yin tries, the more distance will be created between you. There is however potential in this relationship because this is a YinYang fit, which can work if the 4 Yin totally accepts the 8 Yang's Expression allowing it to lead and to set the boundaries but without abuse from the 8 Yang.

Who puts the rubbish out? Definitely the 8 Yang and the 4 Yin should just let it get on with it.

8 with 5:

Friendship: in this combination, both the 5 Yang and 8 Yang will want to lead and control the relationship. As friends or business partners this could work well, as long as you are equal and the goals and what is to be achieved are clear and explicit. In the emotional whirlpool of romantic relationships, this is going to be a lot trickier. It's most likely going to be a battle of wills with neither able nor willing to yield in any meaningful sense.

Who puts the rubbish out? It will probably be a battle with neither prepared to yield.

8 with 6:

Parent - Child: these are two Yang Expressions with the 6 Yang being the child to the 8 Yang parent. There is a mutual understanding here and for the majority of time you should be able to communicate well. Because the 6 Yang is a more natural leader, that Expression will probably want to take that role, but the 8 Yang will likely have a different opinion. These are two strong Yang Expressions and you will need space and time apart and to tackle the harder issues calmly and rationally, which might not always be easy.

Who puts the rubbish out? It's likely to be a bit of a battle, but either can.

8 with 7:

Parent - Child: this is a balanced YinYang relationship and has the potential to make a harmonious partnership with a lot of mutual respect and admiration. The 8 Yang will definitely lead the relationship, but there is much give-and-take, and there is balance in that the 7 Yin will be gentle on the outside but strong on the inside; and the 8 Yang who can have a hard and tough exterior but is actually soft deep down. The 8 Yang may become too controlling and end up abusing the 7 Yin, and that will be a calamity for both, but mainly for the 8 Yang.

Who puts the rubbish out? The 8 Yang will; the 7 Yin will be doing other things.

8 with 8:

Friendship: whilst this is a friendship relationship with the mutual understanding of similar people, there is actually not a lot of trust here. This is because in this case, the 8's tendency towards stubbornness, jealously and self-indulgence is reinforced rather than dissipated and if these cannot be controlled by each partner, this is likely to be a challenging relationship. Both will want to lead and set the boundaries and although one or other may yield a little, it probably can't be sustained for long.

Who puts the rubbish out? You'll most likely argue over it.

8 with 9:

Child - Parent: this has the potential to work well, with the 9 Yin being the parent to the 8 Yang child, making for a balanced YinYang match. You will want to help each other and there is a lot of mutual respect for what the other can bring to the relationship with your respective 'weaknesses' being balanced by the other's 'strengths'. The 8 Yang will inevitably lead the relationship, but must be careful not to be too demanding and the 9 Yin not to be too giving.

Who puts the rubbish out? The 8 Yang will, and will be good at it.

9. Fire Expressions

Male to Female:

9 with 1:

Compatible Opposites: this is a balanced relationship, albeit a 'complex' one, with the 9 Yin male and the 1 Yang female. As in all of these types of relationships, the 9 Yin male must understand that she will need space and time away from him and will be the leader in the relationship. He will be more dependent but may hide that by being showy and extroverted. This is likely to be one of those 'opposites attract' relationships but has great potential to be a happy and harmonious one.

Who puts the rubbish out? She will; no problem.

9 with 2:

Parent - Child: here we have a 9 Yin male parent to a 2 Yin female child. Whilst there is a good mix of Expressions here with his flamboyance and showy qualities balanced with her more sober, steady and sincere approach, you both may be 'fooled' into thinking he is Yang. This illusion cannot be sustained and pretty soon she will probably be seeking something more solid and steady, which he will struggle to provide. In turn, he may find her too conservative and 'high maintenance' although probably he is the 'high maintenance' one.

Who puts the rubbish out? Probably she will, he will be too busy playing to the audience.

9 with 3:

Child - Parent: this is a perfectly balanced relationship with the 'complex' Expressions of the 3 Yang female and 9 Yin male. She is also the 'parent' and will provide support and guidance which if sensitively given will be welcomed, but if perceived as instructions will not. She may regard him as 'highly sensitive' but he will want to exert some control and that may be in the passive aggressive sense, if he thinks his wishes are being ignored or even abused. But overall this should be a smooth connection.

Who puts the rubbish out? She will, and he needs to be OK with that.

9 with 4:

Child - Parent: these are two Yin Expressions, with the parent being the 4 Yin female and the child being the 9 Yin male. This could lead to the 4 Yin female being drained or even exhausted by the demands of the flamboyant 9 Yin male. She will probably try to provide direction but he may well not listen. Both may think he should lead the relationship but really neither is going to be very good at it. Whilst there can be great passion here, ultimately though there may not be much substance in the relationship.

Who puts the rubbish out? She probably should; he will be too busy with other things.

9 with 5:

Parent - Child: here we have a 9 Yin male being the parent to the 5 Yang female. This represents a balanced YinYang connection with two 'complex' Expressions and has the potential to being a harmonious relationship. This is because you both recognise the other's strengths are your weakness and vice versa. The 9 Yin male will be an intelligent, intuitive and inspiring partner and will support and give much to the 5 Yang female, liking her energy, discipline and drive. He may be the parent, but he should take her leadership comfortably.

Who puts the rubbish out? She will, but he might every now and then.

9 with 6:

Passive Control: here the 9 Yin male will try to control the 6 Yang female and will make a pretty poor go of it. This will bewilder and frustrate him who may become passively aggressive as a result. In turn, she may get hurt by his behaviour, but will end up doing her own thing anyway and probably not be that impressed by his tendency to be more show than substance.

Sex, Love and Who Puts the Rubbish Out?

There is a 'complex' YinYang connection, so if he is prepared to yield, a degree of harmony can be achieved, but it probably won't be easy.

Who puts the rubbish out? She should, but he'll think he should.

9 with 7:

Passive Inertia: this is where the 9 Yin male will try to control the 7 Yin female and will make an OK job of it but it's not his natural way. You both like to have an expressive even flamboyant lifestyle and are drawn to the same sorts of things. So in the early days, the relationship looks well-set, but as time goes on the differences between you will become more apparent. He will think she's all talk and no substance; and she thinks he's vain and superior and will be unimpressed by his attempts at leadership: concessions are likely to be rare.

Who puts the rubbish out? He will and will want full marks for his style.

9 with 8:

Parent - Child: this has the potential to work well, with the 9 Yin male being the parent to the 8 Yang female child, making for a 'complex' YinYang match. You will want to help each other and there is a lot of mutual respect for what the other can bring to the relationship with your respective 'weaknesses' being balanced by the other's 'strengths'. She will inevitably lead the relationship, but must be careful not to be too demanding and him not to be too giving.

Who puts the rubbish out? She will, and will be good at it.

9 with 9:

Friendship: with two Fire Expressions together, you are likely to be a lively, pleasure-seeking couple, but with both wanting to be the star of the show, tensions are inevitable. Clear communications are essential in all relationships but this one particularly so. You need to be as open and transparent as possible in what you are thinking and avoid making assumptions or assuming what the other one may be thinking. Also, you need to establish

215

as soon as possible who is best suited to lead the relationship and that might tend more towards the male.

Who puts the rubbish out? Either or, but more likely him.

Female to Male:

9 with 1:

Compatible Opposites: this is a completely balanced partnership relationship with the 1 Yang male going towards the 9 Yin female. As you are complete opposites, you will very likely have pretty different views on life and how to live it, which may cause difficulties, as the 1 Yang male tends to be careful and understated whilst the 9 Yin female is impetuous and outspoken. But if you let yourselves go, forget about Learned Convention and live your Natural Expression, this is a complete YinYang fit.

Who puts the rubbish out? He will; no problem.

9 with 2:

Parent - Child: here we have a 9 Yin female parent to a 2 Yin male child. There is a good mix of Expressions here with the 9 Yin female's flamboyance and showy qualities balanced with the more sober, steady and sincere 2 Yin male. However, it is the parent's role to be supportive and nurturing to the child, and in many ways, the roles here are reversed. This could be difficult in a romantic relationship if the respective boundaries are not defined and that may cause problems sustaining the relationship long term.

Who puts the rubbish out? No big issue here who does: probably best to toss a coin.

9 with 3:

Child - Parent: this is a perfectly balanced relationship with the 'simple' Expressions of the 3 Yang male and 9 Yin female. The 3 Yang male is also the 'parent' and will provide support and guidance which if sensitively given will be welcomed, but if perceived as instructions will not. He may regard her as 'high maintenance' and she will want to exert some control, but that may be in the passive aggressive sense if she thinks her wishes are being ignored or even abused. Overall this should be a smooth connection.

Who puts the rubbish out? He will, and both agree that he should.

9 with 4:

Child - Parent: whilst this is two Yin Expressions, there is potential for this combination because the 4 Yin male is in the parental position and his natural gentleness and easy-going manner compliments her flamboyance and keen mind. Both are likely to be OK that he tries to lead the relationship, but he may end up frustrating her when he is indecisive or conversely being stubborn and he may find her demands draining. Whilst there can be great passion here, ultimately though there may not be much substance in the relationship.

Who puts the rubbish out? He will want to, but may tire quite quickly.

9 with 5:

Parent - Child: here we have a 9 Yin female being the parent to the 5 Yang male. This represents a balanced YinYang connection with two 'simple' Expressions and has the potential to being a harmonious relationship. This is because you both recognise the other's strengths are your weakness and vice versa. The 9 Yin female will be an intelligent, intuitive and inspiring partner and will support and give much to the 5 Yang male, liking his energy, discipline and personal control. Despite being the parent, she should take his leadership comfortably.

Who puts the rubbish out? She will tell him it's his responsibility – and she will be right.

9 with 6:

Passive Control: here the 9 Yin female will try to control the 6 Yang male and will make a pretty poor go of it. This will frustrate the 9 Yin female who may become passively aggressive as a result. He's unlikely to take too much notice, will do his own thing anyway and probably not be that impressed by her tendency to be more show than substance. There is a strong YinYang connection, so if the 9 Yin female is prepared to yield, a degree of harmony can be achieved, but it probably won't be easy.

Who puts the rubbish out? He will, but she will try.

9 with 7:

Passive Inertia: this is where the 9 Yin female will try to control the 7 Yin male and really won't be very good at it, as it's not really her natural way. You both like to have an expressive even flamboyant lifestyle and are drawn to the same sorts of things. So in the early days, the relationship looks well-set, but as time goes on the differences between you will become more apparent. She will think he's all talk and no substance, and he will think she's vain and superior: neither is likely to concede much ground.

Who puts the rubbish out? 50/50: but maybe more her than him – just.

9 with 8:

Parent – Child: this has the potential to work well, with the 9 Yin female being the parent to the 8 Yang male child, making for a 'simple' YinYang match. You will want to help each other and there is a lot of mutual respect for what the other can bring to the relationship with your respective 'weaknesses' being balanced by the other's 'strengths'. He will inevitably lead the relationship, but must be careful not to be too demanding and her not to be too giving.

Who puts the rubbish out? He will, and will be good at it.

9 with 9:

Friendship: with two Fire Expressions together, you are likely to be a lively, pleasure-seeking couple, but with both wanting to be the star of the show, tensions are inevitable. Clear communications are essential in all relationships but this one particularly so. You need to be as open and transparent as possible in what you are thinking and avoid making assumptions or assuming what the other one may be thinking. Also, you need to establish

Sex, Love and Who Puts the Rubbish Out?

as soon as possible who is best suited to lead the relationship and that might tend more towards the male.

Who puts the rubbish out? Either or, but more likely him.

Same Sex:

9 with 1:

Compatible Opposites: this is a totally balanced YinYang relationship. If you each live your life as your Natural Expression, this could be a harmonious and rewarding relationship. You would make excellent business partners with your respective strengths and weaknesses being perfectly balanced out. Whilst you both have leadership potential, the 9 Yin is actually better at being the deputy, which works well because the 1 Yang is a natural leader.

Who puts the rubbish out? The 1 Yang will; with the 9 Yin being an excellent No 2.

9 with 2:

Parent - Child: here we have a 9 Yin parent to a 2 Yin child. Whilst there is a good mix of Expressions here with the 9 Yin's flamboyance and showy qualities balanced with the more sober, steady and sincere 2 Yin, both may be fooled that the 9 Yin's behaviour is Yang. This cannot be sustained and pretty soon the 2 Yin will probably be seeking something more solid and steady which the other will struggle to provide. The 9 Yin may also find the 2 Yin being too conservative and 'high maintenance' although probably you can both fit into that category.

Who puts the rubbish out? Possibly the 2 Yin being the one which actually gets things done.

9 with 3:

Child - Parent: this is a balanced YinYang relationship, where the 3 Yang is the 'parent' and will provide support and guidance to the 9 Yin, which if sensitively given will be welcomed, but if perceived as instructions will not. The 3 Yang may regard the 9 Yin as highly sensitive, but the 9 Yin will want to exert some control, but that may be in the passive aggressive sense, if it thinks its wishes are being ignored or even abused. Overall this should be a smooth connection.

Who puts the rubbish out? The Yang will, and that will be fine for both.

9 with 4:

Child - Parent: these are two Yin Expressions, with the parent being the 4 Yin and the child being the 9 Yin. This could lead to the 4 Yin being drained or even exhausted by the demands of the flamboyant 9 Yin. The 4 Yin will probably try to provide direction but the 9 Yin may well not listen. Both may think that the 4 Yin should lead the relationship but really neither is going to be very good at it. Whilst there can be great passion here, ultimately though there may not be much substance in the relationship.

Who puts the rubbish out? The 4 Yin; the 9 Yin will be too busy with other things.

9 with 5:

Parent - Child: here we have a 9 Yin being the parent to the 5 Yang. This represents a YinYang connection and has the potential to being a harmonious relationship. This is because you both recognise the other's strengths are your weakness and vice versa. The 9 Yin will be an intelligent, intuitive and inspiring partner and will support and give much to the 5 Yang, liking its energy, discipline and drive. The Yin should take the Yang's leadership comfortably.

Who puts the rubbish out? The Yang will, but the Yin might every now and then.

9 with 6:

Passive Control: here the 9 Yin will try to control the 6 Yang and will make a pretty poor go of it. This will bewilder and frustrate the 9 Yin who may become passively aggressive as a result. The 6 Yang may get hurt by this behaviour, but will end up doing its own thing anyway and probably not be that impressed by the 9 Yin's tendency to be more show than substance. There is a YinYang connection, so if the 9 Yin is prepared to yield, a degree of harmony can be achieved, but it probably won't be easy.

Who puts the rubbish out? The Yang will, but the Yin may think it should.

9 with 7:

Passive Inertia: this is where the 9 Yin will try to control the 7 Yin and won't be very good at it. You both like to have an expressive even flamboyant lifestyle and are drawn to the same sorts of things. So in the early days the relationship looks well-set but as time goes on the differences between the two of you become more apparent. The 9 Yin will think the 7 Yin is all talk and no substance and the 7 Yin will think the 9 Yin's vain and superior and be unimpressed by its attempts at leadership: neither is likely to concede much ground.

Who puts the rubbish out? 50/50: but maybe more the 9 Yin – just.

9 with 8:

Parent - Child: this has the potential to work well, with the 9 Yin being the parent to the 8 Yang child, making for a balanced YinYang match. You will want to help each other and there is a lot of mutual respect for what the other can bring to the relationship with your respective 'weaknesses' being balanced by the other's 'strengths'. The 8 Yang will inevitably lead the relationship, but must be careful not to be too demanding and the 9 Yin not to be too giving.

Who puts the rubbish out? The 8 Yang will, and will be good at it.

9 with 9:

Friendship: with two Fire Expressions together, you are likely to be a lively, pleasure-seeking couple, but with both wanting to be the star of the show, tensions are inevitable. Clear communications are essential in all relationships, but this one particularly so. You need to be as open and transparent as possible in what you are thinking and avoid making assumptions or assuming what the other one may be thinking. Also, you need to establish as soon as possible who will be leading the relationship.

Who puts the rubbish out? Either/ or, but you need to agree quickly.

AND FINALLY...

My motives when I first thought about writing this book were for it to be a sort of 'high-end' calling card to help me develop my Practice – I'm hoping it still will be. But sadly, and I'm still a little bewildered by this, the person who first got me on the road to this philosophy wasn't exactly pleased when I told him I was writing this book: in fact, the complete opposite. He had his reasons and that is fine of course, but I mention this only because I am, and always will be, eternally grateful for the gift he brought me. It reminds me of the Picasso quote: "The meaning of life is to find your gift. The purpose of life is to give it away". By contrast, everyone else was very encouraging and supportive. I think that is because whenever I talked it through, they could not only feel my real passion and belief but also that it was a philosophy that made sense, and that it worked!

But as I got further into the book and the more I researched and discussed it with others, I realised that my principle motives had in fact changed. In the same way that I teach a style of yoga that I personally would like to practice, this is a book that I would like to read and a philosophy I'd like to follow. And even if I were to be the only person who ever did, it wouldn't matter, because writing it has helped me to better understand myself and who I really am; whilst at the same time giving me insight and clarity to the people around me and what's going on for them. The result has given me much comfort and peace and provided me with the tools to live my life in a more accepting, loving and kind way. So if only one other person were to feel the same, then as far as I'm concerned, I have given my gift away!

REFERENCES

Christopher Ryan and Cacilda Jetha (2010): Sex At Dawn: How We Mate, Why we Stray, and What It Means for Modern Relationships. New York. Harper Collins ISBN 978-0-06-170780

U G Krishnamurti (2007): Mind Is A Myth: Disquieting Conversations with the Man Called U.G. Boulder. Sentient ISBN 978-1-59181-065-0

John Gray (1992): Men are from Mars, Women are from Venus. New York, Harper Collins ISBN 978-0-060574215

BIBLIOGRAPHY

Jon Sandifer (1997): Feng Shui Astrology: using 9 Star Ki to Achieve Harmony & Happiness in Your Life. London. Piatkus Books 1997 ISBN 0-7499-1709-1

Robert Sachs (2001): Nine Star Ki: Feng Shui Astrology For Deepening Self-Knowledge and Enhancing Relationships, Health and Prosperity. Indiana. iUniverse Books ISBN 978-0-595-5319-4

Takashi Yoshikawa (2007): The Chinese Birthday Book: How to use the Secrets of Ki-ology to Find Love, Happiness, and Success. San Francisco. Red Wheel/Weiser ISBN 10: 1-57863-392-3

David Nassim (2010): The Nature of Classical Chinese Medicine: the foundational context to re-unite myriad styles. Stone. HI Publishing ISBN 978-0-9566873-3-3

WHAT NEXT?

To discuss any of the issues raised in this book, please contact me via my website: www.sexloveandwhoputstherubbishout.com

Here you will also find details of how you can arrange a consultation either face-to-face or via Skype or sign up to a Webinar or a Workshop.

And the site has a number of fun products you can purchase such as t-shirts, mugs and cards.

Thank you to:
Alison C
Caroline C
David E
Jacqui F
Jamna O
Jim R
Pam L
Pauline F
Rachel E
Ruth D
Shona M
Sue C
and to everyone else who has helped, supported and encouraged me on this amazing journey.

ABOUT THE AUTHOR

Rick Nunn has been studying traditional Chinese medicine for many years, and he counsels individuals and couples about their Natural Expression and how that affects their romantic, personal, and professional relationships. Rick lives near London, England with his dog Elsa, where he teaches yoga and holds his 9-Energy Natural Expression practice.